Thankful

KAREN MOORE

Thankful

Practicing the
GRACE of GRATITUDE

52
Weekly
Devotions

Abingdon Press / *Nashville*

THANKFUL

PRACTICING THE GRACE OF GRATITUDE

ISBN 978-1-4267-5522-3

12 13 14 15 16 17 18 19 20 21—10 9 8 7 6 5 4 3 2 1
MANUFACTURED IN THE UNITED STATES OF AMERICA

To my friends and family,
the people who cause my heart to rejoice in gratitude
for the infinite blessings of God

Contents

Introduction

The unthankful heart... discovers no mercies; but let the thankful heart sweep through the day and, as the magnet finds the iron, so it will find, in every hour, some heavenly blessings!
—Henry Ward Beecher

Stop! Don't read this book! Instead, digest it, adopt it as a lifestyle, and bring it to mind each day of the year because every day you always have a reason to be thankful. Every day, God rejoices when you come before him with an attitude of praise. As the psalmist says, you may not be able to publicly recount all the reasons you want to praise him, but you will know in the stillness of your heart that you want to share the joy of all that is good in your life. You want to offer him continual thanks and praise.

This book brings you the opportunity to begin a journey of gratitude, not grousing to the Lord about what you want or what you don't have but, instead, offering him a heart of love for the things you do have, or the things that fill you with peace and contentment. You'll get a little extra encouragement as you begin each week with some scripture passages to meditate on and ponder. Your gift to yourself, as you record your thoughts and blessings, will be the chance to revisit sweet memories of moments that brought you joy or simply made you grateful to be a precious child of God.

Begin then to focus on just one or two things each day that really make you smile. As you do this, your heart and your life will be enriched and your faith will become stronger. With each expression of gratitude will come an outpouring of further joy. Go ahead; try it today!

Should I wake up tomorrow and discover I am able to have only those things I told God I was grateful for yesterday, then I want to be sure I've said how thankful I am for each of you. May God bless you abundantly!

Karen Moore

Thankful for Each New Day!

Praise the LORD! / Give thanks to the LORD because he is good,
/ because his faithful love endures forever. / Who could possibly
repeat / all of the LORD's mighty acts / or publicly recount all his
praise? / The people who uphold justice, / who always do what
is right, are truly happy!
—Psalm 106:1-3

This is "Be happy" week. With each sunrise, you have a reason to thank God for your life and for the good things you enjoy. The psalmist reminds us that one reason to be happy is simply because God is good. God is good and he is faithful and his love for us goes on forever. Imagine that! No matter what you do, how far off the path you stray, how many times you don't get it right, God is good and faithful and his love for you just keeps going on.

Each morning when you rise and are able to get up out of bed (you already have a reason to be thankful, because you spent the night in a nice, warm bed), you can grin from ear to ear. If you're in the habit of counting your blessings before bed at night, you may want to start early. If God was only going to give you back today, the things you told him you were grateful for last night as you counted your blessings, you probably wouldn't have slept a wink. You'd probably still be counting because you wouldn't want to miss the chance to have the good things in your life continue to surround you. So, take a deep breath and begin again to show God what it means to you to be his grateful child, living in unending grace.

How often do we need to see God's face, hear his voice, feel his touch, know his power?
The answer to all these questions is the same: Every day!
—John Blanchard

Lord, let me see you every day and smile. Let me hold up my hands and offer my grateful heart. Today, I remember…

WEEK 1 / DAY 2: *Setting Priorities*

Order your soul; reduce your wants; live in charity, associate in Christian Community; obey the laws; trust in Providence.
—Augustine of Hippo

Our ancient ancestors may not have set New Year's resolutions or kept goal charts on their calendars, but they clearly set their intentions to live a blessed life. Perhaps they too, aspired to have more grateful hearts.

God's spirit made me; the Almighty's breath enlivens me. —Job 33: 4

Today, Lord, I really want to thank you for…

WEEK 1 / DAY 3: *Start Something*

Do not follow where the path may lead. Go instead where there is no path and leave a trail. —Ralph Waldo Emerson

Starting out with a clean slate means you can carve out a new path, try a different road, give yourself the gift of new experiences. The outcome may bring unexpected treasures and reasons to be more thankful to your Creator.

Your Instruction is my joy! Let me live again so I can praise you!
—Psalm 119:174-75

Today, Lord, I'm so grateful for…

WEEK 1 / DAY 4: *Dream*

Hold fast to dreams, for if dreams die, life is like a broken-winged bird that cannot fly. —Robert Frost

It's okay to let your imagination soar, take flight into all the things that stir your heart with passion and joy. God planted desires in your heart so that you might dream them into being, creating more light to share with others. It's a great day to give thanks for those stirrings in your heart that keep you dreaming with growing.

God speaks in one way, / in two ways, but no one perceives it. In the dream, a vision of the night, / when deep sleep falls upon humans, … then he opens people's ears, … / to turn them from a deed / and to smother human pride. —Job 33:14-17

Lord, I thank you for my dreams…

WEEK 1 / DAY 5: *Letting Go of Yesterday*

When one door closes another door opens; but we so often look so long and so regretfully upon the closed door, that we do not see the ones which open for us. —Alexander Graham Bell

It's good to give God the glory for yesterday, to be grateful for where we've been. The past is a good teacher, but like most teachers, it doesn't mean to hold you back, but simply means to guide you toward the future, toward your dreams.

But this is precisely what is written: God has prepared things for those who love him that no eye has seen, or ear has heard, or that haven't crossed the mind of any human being. —1 Corinthians 2:9

Today, Lord, I thank you for my yesterdays…

WEEK 1 / DAY 6: *The Time Is Now*

*We must use time creatively … and forever realize that the time is
always ripe to do right.* —Martin Luther King, Jr.

Each day is like the beginning of the year, a great opportunity to look at how
you want to invest your time and energy. Will you spend time on things that are
no longer in your hands, or will you spend time holding on and holding up the
chance for a bright future?

*In your perspective a thousand years / are like yesterday past, / like a short period
during the night watch.* —Psalm 90:4

Lord, I thank you for the time you have given me. Help me be wise in the
ways I spend the precious time I have …

WEEK 1 / DAY 7: *Stay Strong*

*Every job is the self-portrait of the person who did it. Autograph
your work with excellence.* —Author unknown

You've got it! You've got the plan, the energy, the time and the strength to
move forward. It's a great day to strut your stuff … for the Lord. Let him know
how grateful you are for new direction and possibility.

By your favor you make us strong / because our shield is the LORD's own.
—Psalm 89:17-18

Lord, I am so grateful for the many ways you strengthen me. Help me be
strong as …

Thankful for Being Uniquely Me!

You are the one who created / my innermost parts; / you knit me together while I was still in my mother's womb. / I give thanks to you / that I was marvelously set apart. /Your works are wonderful—I know that very well.
—Psalm 139:13-14

This week is all about you! That's right, you're actually going to spend time being grateful God designed you just the way you are. It may seem a bit scary, but all that matters is the God of this universe created you in a unique way. He knew exactly who you would be. God imagined the best possible you and wants to help you get there. Since you were designed in his image, he is invested in how you turn out.

When you have children, you look to see how they reflect you. They may have your talent, your skill for cooking, or your sensitivity to life. They have your DNA, and that connects you to them. You have God's Spirit within you, and that connects you to him. He looks for all the ways you reflect him.

As you give thanks this week, remember: you're not a finished project, but a work in progress. You're not a perfect human being, but you're perfectly designed to become all you were meant to be. God has given you many gifts and reveals them to you as you're ready to receive them. Trust him! You're a unique and incredible design!

If we did all the things we are capable of doing, we would literally astound ourselves.
—Thomas Edison

Lord, thank you for making me just as I am…

WEEK 2/ DAY 2: *Slightly Cracked*

Though our private desires are ever so confused, though our private requests are ever so broken, and though our private groanings are ever so hidden from others, yet God sees them, records them, and puts them upon the files of heaven and will one day crown them with glorious answers and returns.
—Thomas Brooks (adapted)

The heavenly Potter molded you and brought you into being and continues to work with you. You just have to be willing to be reshaped and modified. The beauty of being slightly cracked, even somewhat broken, is that he is always able to bring you back to wholeness and joy.

But now, LORD, you are our father. / We are the clay, and you are our potter. / All of us are the work of your hand. —Isaiah 64:8

Lord, I am thankful that you continue to shape and mold me. Especially today, I'm thankful for…

WEEK 2/ DAY 3: *My Face*

Though we travel the world over to find the beautiful, we must carry it with us or we find it not. —Ralph Waldo Emerson

One of the things that makes you so uniquely you is your face. The angle of your chin, the sparkle in your eyes, the glow in your cheeks—all are distinctly yours. You're beautiful in your own way. As Emerson reminds us, to be truly beautiful, to be even more than a pretty or handsome face, is to be a person who is lit from within, radiant because of a heart of love and gratitude.

More than anything you guard, / protect your mind, for life flows from it.
—Proverbs 4:23

Lord, today, I am thankful for my face because…

WEEK 2/ DAY 4: *My Voice*

Kind words can be short and easy to speak but their echoes are truly endless. —Mother Teresa

Have you ever noticed what it means to you to hear a loving voice? A kind voice draws you in heart first and keeps you close, protecting your spirit and dignity. God made you with a unique voice, an ability to share from the heart. Be thankful today for your voice that allows you to guide and communicate so fully with others.

The word of Christ must live in you richly. Teach and warn each other with all wisdom by singing psalms, hymns, and spiritual songs. Sing to God with gratitude in your hearts. —Colossians 3:16

Lord, thank you for giving me a voice to…

WEEK 2/ DAY 5: *Your Arms and Legs*

Hence we must support one another, console one another, mutually help, counsel, and advise. —Thomas à Kempis

You are God's hands and feet. You help someone else simply by reaching out with concern or offering a hug or smile. Every time you show up and lend a helping hand you show his love. Every time you become part of the solution, you remind others that God is good and works through his people on this planet. Be thankful today for your arms and legs.

Be kind, compassionate, and forgiving to each other, in the same way God forgave you in Christ. —Ephesians 4:32

Lord, thank you for my arms and legs…

WEEK 2/ DAY 6: *Your Heart*

When you make that one effort to feel compassion instead of blame or self-blame, the heart opens again and continues opening. —Sara Paddison

One of the extraordinary things about you is the way you share your heart. You offer love and compassion like no one else. God has given you a unique dose of himself so that you can share it. You have a strong heart and you exercise it every time you open it with grace. Be thankful for your generous heart.

Therefore, as God's choice, holy and loved, put on compassion, kindness, humility, gentleness, and patience. Be tolerant with each other and, if someone has a complaint against anyone, forgive each other. —Colossians 3:12-13

Lord, thank you for giving me a compassionate heart to…

WEEK 2/ DAY 7: *Your Eyes*

The most pathetic person in the world is someone who has sight but has no vision. —Helen Keller

When God invited you into his story, he did a miraculous thing. He gave you new eyes, and new ways to see the world. He gave you a vision. Now he leaves it to you to interpret what direction you'll go with the things you see and the ways you'll share the desires of your heart. God gave you beautiful eyes to shine his light on a needy world.

When there's no vision, / the people get out of control, / but whoever obeys instruction is happy. —Proverbs 29:18

Lord, thank you for helping me see…

Thankful for My Life Purpose

So then, let's also run the race that is laid out in front of us, since
we have such a great cloud of witnesses surrounding us.
—Hebrews 12:1

Okay, so you're smiling to yourself because at this very moment, you're not that clear about what your life purpose is. You've stumbled onto pieces of it, working through it like a jigsaw puzzle, hoping to discover the actual picture before too long. If that's the case, then be grateful. Give God thanks that you have gotten this far and that you can actually imagine there really is a purpose to your life, a mission for you to accomplish. The truth is, God designed you intentionally, for a purpose that only you can fulfill in a way that he knew would make you strong and happy. God desires all that is good for you, so your soul resonates with joy and your spirit sings. He knows you so well.

Embrace your mission. Seek to know more of what God would have from you, what God would dream for you. As his beloved child, you can be sure that your life has great meaning to many people. Let your grateful heart lead the way.

God sees every one of us; he creates every soul... for a purpose.
—John Henry Newman

Lord, I thank you for the good work you have begun in me; help me...

WEEK 3/ DAY 2: *Setting a New Goal*

*Set yourself earnestly to discover what you are made to do, and
then give yourself passionately to the doing of it.*
—Martin Luther King, Jr.

Imagine how excited you feel when you set out to explore a new place, a new country, somewhere you have never been. Apply that same principle to discovering more about yourself today. Try things you've never tried before and you may discover a new territory within yourself, a new country. Your life purpose will unfold right before your eyes.

Desire first and foremost God's kingdom and God's righteousness, and all these things will be given to you as well. —Matthew 6:33

Lord, thank you for being with me as I start anew to explore my own world of possibility…

WEEK 3/ DAY 3: *A Positive Attitude*

*It's a beautiful world to see, / Or it's dismal in every zone, / But
the thing it must be in its gloom or its gleam / All depends on you
alone.* —Author unknown

You probably already know that life is not so much what happens to you, but what you do when uncertain and difficult things occur. Your job is to maintain a sense of joyful optimism, knowing you have a goal to accomplish and that no matter what life brings, you will keep working toward that goal. Your spirit and your attitude toward the things you do make all the difference.

Renew the thinking in your mind by the Spirit and clothe yourself with the new person created according to God's image. —Ephesians 4:23-24

Lord, help me see the bright side when it comes to difficult life events…

WEEK 3/ DAY 4: *Making a Good Effort*

Firmness of purpose is one of the most necessary sinews of character, and one of the best instruments for success. Without it, genius wastes its efforts in a maze of inconsistencies. —Chesterfield

If your purpose is to discover what it is that God designed you to become, then Lord Chesterfield's idea may strengthen your resolve. After all, once you've firmly established the goal, making the effort to accomplish the task is definitely the right track. Thank God that he gives you the opportunity to have such singleness of mind.

All who are led by God's Spirit are God's sons and daughters. —Romans 8:14

Lord, thank you for leading me in the effort I'm making toward discovering your purpose for me ...

WEEK 3/ DAY 5: *Some Good Advice*

No gift is more precious than good advice. —Erasmus

In the spirit of discovery, it can be very helpful to check in with trusted friends and advisors, taking into consideration the things they might observe about you that could help you find your way. Thank God for the good people around you who are willing to step out in faith and offer you their heartfelt thoughts and guidance!

Plans fail with no counsel, but with many counselors they succeed.
—Proverbs 15:22

Lord, thank you for the kindness of people who genuinely seek my good and who help me find my way ...

WEEK 3/ DAY 6: *Your Character*

*Out of our beliefs are born deeds; out of our deeds we form habits;
out of our habits grows our character; and on our character we
build our destiny.* —Henry Hancock

Your life purpose comes together through a series of choices and beliefs that
you have about yourself and the world around you. God is there in the midst of
those choices helping you to create a habit of holiness and a heart of gratitude.
With those things he can strengthen you toward your destiny.

Good people bring out good things from their good treasure. —Matthew 12:35

Lord, thank you for helping me develop a strong character to…

WEEK 3/ DAY 7: *With a Little Perseverance*

The secret of success is constancy of purpose.
—Benjamin Disraeli

You're doing well. Even in the effort to persist toward your goal, your heart
opens in gratitude toward the One who keeps you on the path, strengthens
your steps, and helps you move closer to the goal. God has awesome plans for
you, so just keep going.

You need to endure so that you can receive the promises after you do God's will.
—Hebrews 10:36

Lord, thank you for helping me stay the course, for guiding me toward the
goal…

Thankful for Good Friends

Friends love all the time, / and kinsfolk are born for times of trouble.
—*Proverbs 17:17*

Y ou've probably already developed an attitude of gratitude when it comes to your close friends, those you rely on to be there through the cloudbursts and rainbows of life. You're that kind of friend, and so it only makes sense for you to have such supportive people around you as well.

This week, focus on your relationships, especially your authentic friendships. You probably know many people, but only a few of them are genuine friends. Only a few of them are people God put into your life for very specific reasons. He wants to help you reach your life goals and so he provides a valuable support group.

As you thank him for your friends, focus on the unique attributes of a particular friendship that cause it to make such a difference to your life. The best friends will share the gifts of kindness, loyalty, forgiveness, love, and acceptance. Give God the glory for each of them.

True friends don't spend time gazing into each other's eyes. They may show great tenderness towards each other, but they face in the same direction—toward common projects, goals—above all, towards a common Lord. —C. S. Lewis

Lord, I thank you today for my true friends. Please watch over…

WEEK 4/ DAY 2: *Stick Together*

Blessed is the influence of one true, loving soul on another.
—George Eliot

No doubt, your heart swells with gratitude when you think of your closest friends, your allies in the world. You know full well the incredible gifts you share, and the opportunities that have made real friendship blossom. You've stuck together like buffers against the winds of life, strengthening and renewing one another's spirits. Praise and thanksgiving tumble easily from your lips for friendships like these. What a blessing!

There are persons for companionship, but then there are friends who are more loyal than family. —Proverbs 18:24

Lord, thank you so much for my loyal friends, especially…

WEEK 4/ DAY 3: *Ouch! Forgive Me Again!*

Forgiveness doesn't change the past, but it definitely changes the future! —Author unknown

Sometimes the closer you are to another person, the harder it is to be truly forgiving. After all, that person really knows you and you've been through a lot together. Why would either of you do anything to hurt the other? Today, say thank you for those things that have caused you and a friend to have to clear the air and mend the bruises. Give thanks for things that make your friendship even stronger. Let forgiveness cause your relationship to blossom.

Be tolerant with each other and, if someone has a complaint against anyone, forgive each other. —Colossians 3:13

Father, thank you for the opportunity forgiveness brings to my relationship with…

WEEK 4/ DAY 4: *Loving You Just the Way You Are!*

Jesus accepts you the way you are, but loves you too much to leave you that way. —Lee Venden

You're already grateful for those friends who seem to accept you just as you are, who love you no matter what mood might be carrying you through a day. These are the same friends who will express honest opinions and heartfelt thoughts about your life. Life just wouldn't be the same without them. Today, give God a big shout out for the friends who keep you going no matter what.

Those who refresh others will themselves be refreshed. —Proverbs 11:25b

Lord, thank you for the friends who accept me just as I am. Thank you for…

WEEK 4/ DAY 5: *A Little Hospitality*

To give our Lord a perfect hospitality, Mary and Martha must combine. —Teresa of Avila

You're probably a great host when friends come to call. Your house is homey and tidy, you've baked a special delight to cause a slight stir of joy, and it all feels good. It pleases God when you find little moments to share with those you love, when you have a chance to be fully engaged in the simple festivities of life. On behalf of Mary, though, send some special thanks to God for those precious moments.

Keep loving each other like family. Don't neglect to open up your homes to guests, because by doing this some have been hosts to angels without knowing it.
—Hebrews 13:1-2

Lord, I love having my friends over at my house. Thank you for…

WEEK 4/ DAY 6: *Friends Hold Up the Light*

Sometimes our light goes out but is blown into flame by another human being. Each of us owes deepest thanks to those who have rekindled this light. —Albert Schweitzer

It's not always easy to keep your light shining. A good friend may not always know how to fix whatever is going on in your life that has caused you to feel mildly depressed or more interested in hiding out than shining anywhere. Even without the answers you need, a good friend reminds you that the light is still there, just up ahead. Thank God for the light of good friends.

As water reflects the face, so the heart reflects one person to another. —Proverbs 27:19

Lord, I'm so thankful for the way my friends support me, holding me up and helping me see the light of possibility…

WEEK 4/ DAY 7: *Friends Hear Your Heart*

His thoughts were slow, / His words were few and never formed to glisten. / But he was a joy to all his friends, / You should have heard him listen! —Author unknown

Three cheers for friends who know how to listen to what you say, and even what you don't say. These are the ones who listen from the heart and receive you with love. God listens to you in that way too, so thank him for hearing your heart and not just your words. Thank him for the gift of those who take time to listen.

Everyone should be quick to listen, slow to speak, and slow to grow angry. —James 1:19

Lord, thank you for those precious few friends who truly hear my heart…

Thankful for My Home

∽◦◦◦◦◦∾

*A wise woman builds her house, / while a foolish woman tears
hers down with her own hands.*
—Proverbs 14:1

It's easy to take the laundry, the dishes, and the dusting for granted, but the truth is, those things should give you a happy face. Those things remind you of what it means to have a home, a sanctuary, a place to call your own. In a world where millions of people are homeless, it's more appropriate than ever to give God thanks and praise for our homes.

As you go through this week, imagine a soldier far away, missing his home and family, and offer thanks for his work and the safe place you call home because of him. Imagine the person torn apart by job losses and economic crisis and a home in foreclosure. When you imagine things like these, you realize that you have been blessed in a big way.

God has blessed you beyond measure. Whether your home is an apartment in the city, a mansion in the countryside, or a house that looks like every other house on the block, it's your space, your place where everybody welcomes you back again, no matter how far away you might go. Wherever life takes you this week, give thanks each time you walk through your door, for there truly is "no place like home."

*In ordinary life we hardly realize that we receive a great deal more than we give, and
that it is only with gratitude that life becomes rich.* —Dietrich Bonhoeffer

Thank you for the home you have blessed me with…

WEEK 5/ DAY 2: *Of Stoves, Refrigerators, and Dishes in the Sink*

Each small task of everyday life is part of the total harmony of the universe. —Thérèse of Lisieux

Give thanks today for the small tasks, the chance to make your favorite dinner, bake a cake, or smell glorious temptations from your own oven. What a joy it is to know that you can go to your own kitchen, cupboards full of possibilities, ready to become works of art by your own hand. Thank God for your kitchen!

Don't forget to do good and to share what you have because God is pleased with these kinds of sacrifices. —Hebrews 13:16

Lord, I do thank you that I can create whatever I want in my humble kitchen…

WEEK 5/ DAY 3: *A Moment for Myself*

Little things console us because little things afflict us.
—Blaise Pascal

Thank God today for that special spot in your house that causes you to relax, slip away from the world, and rest in his love. It may be your big old easy chair; it may be a soothing warm bath; or it may just be when you wrap yourself in an old comfy sweater. Be thankful that you have something that brings you such sweet bliss.

When my anxieties multiply, your comforting calms me down. —Psalm 94:19

Lord, thank you for those precious moments when I can relax and simply be myself…

WEEK 5/ DAY 4: *Showers of Goodness*

Blissful are the simple, for they shall have much peace.
—Thomas à Kempis

Can there be anything quite as rewarding, quite as simple, or as lovely as a good warm shower? It is poised to wash away the grief of yesterday, to renew the spirit within you, and to send you back into the world with a clean slate, ready to take on all that comes your way. Thank God and imagine him pouring out his generous spirit on you for a new start today.

He [God] did it through the washing of new birth and the renewing by the Holy Spirit, which God poured out upon us generously through Jesus Christ our Savior. —Titus 3:5-6

Lord, thank you for renewing my spirit…

WEEK 5/ DAY 5: *Comfy, Cozy Bed*

We have within ourselves enough to fill the present day with joy, and overspread the future years with hope.
—William Wordsworth

Early to bed and early to rise, may make you healthy, wealthy, and wise, or it may simply make you thankful that you have such a wonderful place to lay your head. Take a moment today to thank God for your clean sheets, your warm blankets, and your soft pillows. If you have those things, you have a luxury that much of the world does not have. Enjoy your blessings today.

Give thanks in every situation because this is God's will for you in Christ Jesus.
—1 Thessalonians 5:18

Lord, whether it's crawling into bed after a long day, or rising from its comfort in the morning, I thank you…

WEEK 5/ DAY 6: *Grace for the Day*

A happy family is but an earlier heaven. —John Bowring

If you have a family that says a prayer at mealtime, offering thanks for the food God has provided, that is in itself a reason to be grateful. If you don't have a family that prays, but you have one that comes together in love and shares the gifts of the day, then you still have reason to be grateful. In truth, any time you share a meal with others, they are your family for that moment and that alone gives you the opportunity to offer your own thanks and praise.

God settles the lonely in their homes. —Psalm 68:6

Lord, thank you for the people who share meals with me.

WEEK 5/ DAY 7: *Front Porch Memories*

There is no principle of the heart that is more acceptable to God than a universal, ardent love for all mankind, which seeks and prays for their happiness. —William Law

Do you remember when people had front porches, places where they could connect with the neighbors and discover more about each other's lives? You may not have a front porch anymore, but you are a neighbor and someone in your hometown is grateful you're there—your neighbors.

Let the people thank you, God! Let all the people thank you! —Psalm 67: 5

Lord, I am so grateful for my neighbors because…

Thankful for the Mamas and the Papas

*Honor your father and your mother so that your life will be long
on the fertile land that the LORD your God is giving you.*
—*Exodus 20:12*

Though we may indeed be thankful for that once popular folk group who encouraged us to "hammer out the love between our brothers and our sisters all over this land," this week honors our real parents or those who parented us as we were growing and learning and being shaped into worthy adults. You may find that your "real" parents were not your biological parents, but people who truly inspired your direction, encouraged your heart and mind, and offered you some nuggets of truth to carry on your way.

Parents really are special people. They may have understood the gravity and the joy of their influence and importance in your life or they may have missed more opportunities to connect with you than either of you care to revisit. The fact remains that God wants us to honor our parents and in so doing, give thanks for them.

With heartfelt gratitude, lift up your parents and thank them for simply being who they are, the people who brought you into the world, the people who protected your life and spirit, and the people who graciously served to inspire your path. God, bless parents everywhere.

Be the soul support of your children. —Author unknown

Lord, thank you for my parents and others who mentor and influence children the world over…

WEEK 6/ DAY 2: *Care and Feeding*

There is nothing in a caterpillar that tells you it's going to be a butterfly. —Buckminster Fuller

Just like that cocoon that surrounds the caterpillar providing safety and nutrients so that a beautiful butterfly may one day emerge, so it is with parenting. Parents provide life's basic necessities to ensure the most beautiful emergence of a successful adult, with both roots and wings. Give thanks for all your parents did to nurture you today.

Who among you will give your children a stone when they ask for bread? —Matthew 7:9

Lord, I truly thank you for my parents…

WEEK 6/ DAY 3: *For Loving Examples*

When you lead your sons and daughters in the good way, let your words be tender and caressing, in terms of discipline that wins the heart's assent. —Elijah Ben Soloman Zalman

In our growing-up years, we often go from believing our parents know absolutely everything, to being amazed that they somehow have lost their minds and no longer know anything. What a gift it is to discover that they are simply doing their best at any given moment to listen, to speak, and to guide their children. Thank God today for those moments when you were able to hear, able to accept, and ready to embrace the wisdom your parents provided.

Listen to your father, who gave you life; don't despise your elderly mother. —Proverbs 23:22

Lord, I thank you for all that I learned from my parents' example and love…

WEEK 6/ DAY 4: *Thanks for the Discipline?*

When God chastises his children, he does not punish as a judge does; but he chastens as a father. —C. H. Spurgeon

You may not have always thought your parents were fair in their approaches to discipline. You may have wanted desperately to disobey them, and yet, today, you may also reflect on a time you didn't understand, but with adult eyes, see it for what it was, a moment to be shaped and pruned, loved in a different way. Thank God for the parents who cared enough to discipline you with love!

Discipline your children while there is hope. —Proverbs 19:18

Lord, I did not always understand the way my parents chose to discipline me, but I thank you anyway for the ways my life has been shaped…

WEEK 6/ DAY 5: *In Praise of Teachers*

Our critical day is not the very day of our death, but the whole course of our life; I thank them that pray for me when my bell tolls; but I thank them much more, that catechize me, or preach to me, or instruct me how to live. —John Donne

Parents offer you the first window of education. Either from example or by direct learning, you soak in the world. You observe with curious eyes, then crawl into discovery, only to eventually stand on our own and run at a pace you design yourself. Thanks to your parents who were great teachers in every possible way.

Listen to advice and accept instruction, so you might grow wise in the future. —Proverbs 19:20

Clearly, Lord, I am thankful for the guidance and instruction I received from my parents…

WEEK 6/ DAY 6: *No Place Like Home*

There is nothing like staying at home for real comfort.
—Jane Austen

It may well be true that home is "where you hang your heart," because most of us always long to go "home" wherever we imagine home to be. Parents who provided a home that was warm and inviting, nurturing and caring are to be praised beyond measure. Thank your parents today for giving you that sense of belonging, the joy of knowing the gifts of home.

All around your table, your children will be like olive trees, freshly planted./ That's how it goes for anyone / who honors the LORD: / they will be blessed! —Psalm 128:3-4

Lord, thank you for providing me with a home that taught me...

WEEK 6/ DAY 7: *Learning to Play*

Wherever they go, and whatever happens to them on the way, in that enchanted place on the top of the Forest, a little boy and his Bear will always be playing.
—A. A. Milne, closing lines of *The House at Pooh Corner*

Thanks to your parents for a home that gave you a place to play. You may have built forts or jumped in the raked leaves. You may have played vicariously through books and the characters you grew to love. You learned that you could enjoy being with those you loved and simply embracing moments of family pleasures.

The city will be full of boys and girls playing in its plazas. —Zechariah 8:5

Lord, thank you for providing the down-time, the just-be-myself time, the time to simply play and relax...

Thankful for the Awesome Examples of Jesus

*So live in Christ Jesus the Lord in the same way as you received
him. Be rooted and built up in him, be established in faith, and
overflow with thanksgiving just as you were taught.*
—Colossians 2:6-7

At the very name of Jesus, our hearts swell with gratitude and with awe for
all that he has done. He committed himself to us and remains faithful for
all eternity. That alone inspires us to rejoice. If we go back to the very beginning,
John reminds us that he was with God, part of the Supreme Godhead creating
a place for you and me.

As we look at the brief life of Jesus, one that has never been matched in its
effect and influence on others, it's hard to imagine why he loves us so much.
The facts are clear, though: for God so loved the world, he gave his only Son,
and with that, he allows us to also be sons and daughters. If we begin now, we
will run out of time to offer sufficient praise for that fact alone.

God so loved the world, and God so loved you, he provided a Shepherd, a
King, a Lamb, and a Savior. He provided examples of how to live and how to
love and how to become more of what God designed you to be. Thank God
for his incredible plan and his amazing and worthy Son, Jesus.

Definition of a Christian—Under New Management —Author unknown

Dear Lord, I realize that I barely understand what you have done to give me
life, but I thank you…

WEEK 7/ DAY 2: *Jesus Heals the Broken Me*

*A broken body and a broken heart have only One source, One
healer to make them whole again.* —Karen Moore

Sometimes life is a pain! Your body gets run down or shuts down or simply
rebels for reasons that may not seem logical. Your heart gets broken by love or
loss, by rejection or loneliness. Nothing seems to make sense and no prayer
seems to find an answer that causes your spirit to rise again. There is yet one
avenue for you. Give thanks and praise for the great Physician, the Healer of
hurts and pains, no matter how big or how small. His RX is always the same and
it's created with love.

*Then they begged him that they might just touch the edge of his clothes. Everyone
who touched him was cured.* —Matthew 14:36

Lord, thank you for healing me of…

WEEK 7/ DAY 3: *Jesus Loves Me, This I Know!*

*The love of Christ is like the blue sky, into which you may see
clearly, but the real vastness of which you cannot measure.*
—Robert Murray McCheyne

Look up—beyond the flying birds and clouds, beyond the things you can
see, and keep looking. If you look long enough, you may get a glimpse of
heaven, and begin to realize the depth and breadth and vastness of the love
Jesus has for you. Now hum a little or sing out loud, "Jesus loves me, this I
know!" Keep singing until the "This I KNOW" part is embedded in your spirit.
Your heart will overflow with gratitude.

We love because God first loved us. —1 John 4:19

Lord, thank you for your faithfulness and love…

WEEK 7 / DAY 4: *My Daily Bread*

Where God guides, he provides. —Author unknown

God knows what you need. He sees you from a vantage point that even you cannot understand. Yet, each day, each moment, he supplies what you need for now. He knows the details that will make a difference to you. Give God the glory today.

We know that God works all things together for good for the ones who love God, for those who are called according to his purpose. —Romans 8:28

God, thank you for your continual provision, and for the guidance that you so faithfully give…

WEEK 7 / DAY 5: *Jesus Is My Flashlight!*

And I said to the man who stood at the gate of the year: "Give me a light that I may tread safely into the unknown." And he replied: "Go out into the darkness and put your hand into the hand of God. That shall be to you better than light, and safer than a known way." —Minnie L. Haskins

When it's not easy to see where you're going, your heart longs for a light, a beacon that will guide you safely to your next destination. Praise God for the many ways he shines a light on your life, offering both hope and guidance. He is your flashlight, the lamp of possibility.

Your word is a lamp before my feet and a light for my journey. —Psalm 119:105

God, thank you for always providing the perfect light…

WEEK 7/ DAY 6: *He Knows Me Inside Out*

Human things must be known to be loved: but Divine things must be loved to be known. —Blaise Pascal

Your human story began at birth, but your heavenly story began when God first conceived you out of his great love for you. He knew you before you were even a speck of humanity. He knew you and created a space for you to find your way back to him. Isn't it awesome to imagine what great and intentional love he has for you? Thank him with a grateful heart today.

You are the one who created / my innermost parts; / you knit me together while I was still in my mother's womb./ I give thanks to you / that I was marvelously set apart. —Psalm 139:13-14

Lord, I know that no one knows me like you do…

WEEK 7/ DAY 7: *He Gives Me a Clean Slate*

The house of my soul is too small for you to come to it. May it be enlarged by you. It is in ruins, restore it. —Augustine of Hippo

Sometimes we need a do-over, a chance to get it right or at least get it better. Jesus offers us a clean slate every morning, making all things new and giving us a chance to be restored. Like Augustine's, our hearts may not be sufficiently enlarged to contain all that God has for us. Thank God today that he chooses to dwell with you and to breathe new life into you any time you ask.

But "when God our savior's kindness and love appeared, he saved us because of his mercy, not because of righteous things we had done." —Titus 3:4-5

Father, I thank you that you give me a new chance each day to…

Thankful for the Little Things

❧

*I came so that they could have life—indeed, so that they could
live life to the fullest.*
—John 10:10

Whoever said, "Little things mean a lot" had it right. We may dream and
hope for the big things, but it's the smaller, inconsequential things that
keep us going and trying harder. You may not wake up each morning and
thank God that you can see the world with your sleepy eyes, or that you can
smell the coffee already beckoning you to rise and shine. You may not give
thanks that you have a bar of soap to wash your hands or a small kitten who
rubs "good morning" purrs against your leg.

If we started to thank God for all the little things each morning, we'd be well
into the afternoon before we could pause to take a breath. Perhaps this is the
way we can pray without ceasing. Perhaps each time we give thanks that we
exist right where we are in heartfelt prayer, we start to become wiser. We start
to see the real picture of our lives and how it is we truly live an abundant life.
Jesus came to give us abundant life and he offers us showers of goodness each
day in the little things we enjoy. Hallelujah!

A life in thankfulness releases the glory of God. —Bengt Sundberg

Lord, you've provided a wealth of simple things for me to enjoy. Thank you
for…

WEEK 8/ DAY 2: *Cups of Joy*

Our life is simply frittered away by detail. Simplify. Simplify.
—Henry David Thoreau

Whether you enjoy a steaming cup of hot coffee, a delightful frappuccino, or some sweet herb tea, there's nothing quite as lovely as taking a break. The details of life can stress the soul and rob the spirit of true joy. Simplify your life whenever you can and thank God for those quiet, more peaceful moments when you savor the goodness of all he does for you.

Aim to live quietly, mind your own business, and earn your own living.
—1 Thessalonians 4:11

Lord, thank you for those splendid moments to enjoy…

WEEK 8/ DAY 3: *Color My World*

Red for His shed blood He paid, / Green is grass, so sweetly laid. /
Yellow is the sun so bright, / Orange is the edge of night./
Black for sins we try to hide, /White because we are His bride. /
Purple for His royalty / Pink for joy that sets us free./
Colors in a rainbow sky / That mean far more than meets the eye.
—Karen Moore

How wonderful that God has created the world with such richness of color, vibrant and living, joyful and subdued. Each color evokes a mood, a feeling, a sense of something greater than itself. Thank God for his faithful brush, his bold palette, and his brilliant artistry today.

Everything came into being through the Word, and without the Word nothing came into being. —John 1:3

Lord, thank you for creating such a vibrant, beautiful world…

WEEK 8/ DAY 4: *It's Electrifying!*

Faith is like electricity. You can't see it, but you can see the light.
—Author unknown

When the electricity goes off, we realize how much we depend on it. After all, we suddenly are out of touch with the world without the internet, or we're perhaps without heat or water or cell phone service. Our world no longer lights up beyond a candle glow. Electricity, like love, and maybe like faith, is something we might take for granted. Thank God, he's already plugged you into his system and through him all things are possible.

All things are possible for the one who has faith. —Mark 9:23

Father, I thank you today for electricity because...

WEEK 8/ DAY 5: *Planes, Trains, and My Little Chevy*

Wandering re-establishes the original harmony which once existed between man and the universe. —Anatole France

Thank God that now and then he forces you out of your comfort zone. He packs your bags and gives you a GPS to a new destination. Sometimes he wants to get in touch with you in a new way and the best avenue is to put you somewhere away from those old familiar places. He loves to see you get up and go. On your next trip to the grocery store or across the world, thank him that you are on the move.

You will seek the LORD your God from there, and you will find him if you seek him with all your heart and with all your being. —Deuteronomy 4:29

Lord, thank you for the gift of transportation and the opportunity to...

WEEK 8/ DAY 6: *The Book Hook*

Many people, other than the authors, contribute to the making of a book, from the first person who had the bright idea of alphabetic writing through the inventor of movable type to the lumberjacks who felled the trees that were pulped for its printing. It is not customary to acknowledge the trees themselves, though their commitment is total. —Forsyth and Rada, *Machine Learning*

We seldom stop to thank all those who contribute so well to the books we read. The same principle applies to the clothes we wear, the food we eat, and the car we drive. The product, the end result, is only ours by virtue of hundreds of others who deserve our thanks and gratitude. God may have created all things with a committee of three, but everything else in the world took hundreds of helpful hands. Thank God for all those hands today.

In God we live, move, and exist. —Acts 17:28

Lord, thank you for all the things that bring me joy, the books I read and…

WEEK 8/ DAY 7: *Information Blitzkrieg*

We cannot live only for ourselves. A thousand fibers connect us with our fellow men. —Herman Melville

If the internet does anything, it reminds us that God was definitely in the details. If we can gather more information than we can possibly stick into our brains in ten minutes of searching, we might begin to see how intricate and delicate his work has been. It's good to be thankful for technology, thankful for the opportunity to connect so easily with neighbors and friends, and thankful that we can begin to see how big our God really is.

God said to Moses, "I Am Who I Am. So say to the Israelites, 'I Am has sent me to you.'" —Exodus 3:14

Lord, every generation finds new ways to learn of you, to connect to all that is. Thank you for…

Thankful for Love

❦

*Love should be shown without pretending. Hate evil, and hold on
to what is good. Love each other like the members of your family.*
—Romans 12:9-10

Love is constantly playing its song somewhere. Sometimes the music is soft
and gentle, causing the heart to flutter in the stillness. Sometimes it's loud
and boisterous like a symphony in the park on a warm summer day. Other
times, it seems cold, worn-out, almost lifeless because it's been bullied and
beaten and provoked in ways that were never meant to speak its name. God is
love and we may struggle with what that means when love seems so fleeting in
our lives. We may wonder how to imagine love when it trickles through our fin-
gers like coins in a slot machine. The fact remains that life is built on a foundation of love. That's what God's love is, a foundation of goodness and possibility,
a place to start or start over when love is elusive.

This week be thankful for love in several of its forms, thankful that you recognize it when it comes to you and that you share it in full measure when it
quickens your pulse. Love isn't looking for pretenders. It's looking for authen-
ticity, openness, and generosity. Love wants to come home to you every day.
Thank God!

God's love is unconditional. Is yours? —Author unknown

Lord, thank you for the love you've placed in my heart. Help me…

WEEK 9/ DAY 2: *Music for the Soul*

What's love with all its art, verse, music, worth compared with love, found, gained and kept? —Robert Browning

Love inspires poets and songwriters, filmmakers and preachers. It lifts the hearts of those who are willing to ponder it, live within its grasp, and embrace its truth. Love gives us every reason to be grateful. How wonderful it is to know that we have a God in heaven who sees us and loves us right where we are. God be praised!

Rushing waters cannot quench love; rivers can't wash it away. —Song of Songs 8:7

Lord, for those I have loved and who have loved me in return, I thank you…

WEEK 9/ DAY 3: *Giving and Receiving*

You can give without loving, but you cannot love without giving. —Amy Carmichael

What if we were filled with such generosity of spirit and love that others were energized, inspired, and renewed simply by the fact that we passed by? Perhaps then, even touching the hem of our garment could make a difference. That is how we are loved, by the One who gives even before we ask. Give thanks for all the ones who are lovingly generous to you.

It is more blessed to give than to receive. —Acts 20:35

Lord, thank you for your generosity and for all those who…

WEEK 9/ DAY 4: *In the Service of Love*

Those prepared to do love's service will receive her rewards: new comfort and new strength. —Hadewijch

Motivated by love, we look for the small things we can do, clues to another's happiness. God does the same for us. He seeks to know us so well that he can share little moments, little gifts through the voices and the hugs of others that will remind us again and again that he is there. We serve him and each other in humble gratitude.

Whoever serves should do so from the strength that God furnishes. —1 Peter 4:11

Thank you, Lord, for those who serve my needs so well with kindness and love, especially…

WEEK 9/ DAY 5: *Time after Time*

In the time we have it is surely our duty to do all the good we can to all the people we can in all the ways we can.
—William Barclay

We're grateful for those who love us so much they give us the best gift of all— their time. They honor us with their presence, strengthening our spirits. Love looks for ways to share, time after time after time. God seeks to know our love in the same way, seeking time with us so that we can share intimate conversations as good friends do. Thank God for those who take the time to love you well.

Don't be in debt to anyone, except for the obligation to love each other. —Romans 13:8

It's a wonder, Lord, that those I love so often seek my time and attention, and I thank you…

WEEK 9/ DAY 6: *A Little Romance*

Let us be grateful to people who make us happy, they are the charming gardeners who make our souls blossom.
—Marcel Proust

Most of us blossom under the watchful eye of someone who seeks our good and makes us feel happy. Sneaking a love note into a lunch box or calling with a quick note of love before heading out for the day plants seeds of joy like nothing else can. Love helps us grow strong and healthy. Be thankful for those who are the sunshine that helps your soul blossom.

Pursue love. —1 Corinthians 14:1

Lord, thank you for the little gems that love brings, especially for…

WEEK 9/ DAY 7: *He Said, She Said*

My wife said I never listen to her. At least I think that's what she said. —Author unknown

We appreciate those who take the time to listen to us, to really hear and weigh our thoughts. It's so important to know we've been heard. Love listens. No doubt, God understands this need in us and in our relationships since he so often said, "Let the one who has ears to hear, hear." Thank him for those who truly listen to your heart and mind.

Everyone who has ears should pay attention. —Matthew 13:9

Lord, thank you that you are always so willing to hear me, and thank you for…

Thankful for Prayer

In the same way, the Spirit comes to help our weakness. We don't know what we should pray, but the Spirit himself pleads our case with unexpressed groans. The one who searches hearts knows how the Spirit thinks, because he pleads for the saints, consistent with God's will.
—*Romans 8:26-27*

The whole idea of prayer is awesome! We think it's amazing that we can tap into the internet and connect with millions of people at once, or one person at a time, and yet we still don't get what prayer is. Prayer is a powerful connection between you and God, and it never fails. It never goes down, it never gets interrupted. Prayer plugs you into the greatest Source of power and energy possible, the Creator of all things.

Saying we appreciate the idea of prayer is nice. Getting the awesome opportunity we have to speak directly to the King of the Universe, the Lord of All, the I AM, is beyond our comprehension and yet, prayers go up to the kingdom every second of the day and each prayerful voice is heard. Each one is valued. Each one reminds God that he has people on earth who seek a relationship with him. Thank God each time you bow your head, or send a hopeful and prayerful thought his way. He hears you!

To get back on your feet, get down on your knees. —Author unknown

Lord, thank you for hearing me. Thank you for connecting to my needs and wants and spirit in this way. Especially today, I pray for …

WEEK 10/ DAY 2: *For Wisdom*

If you realize that you aren't as wise today as you thought you were yesterday, you're wiser today. —Author unknown

Whether experience actually provides the opportunity to grow in wisdom, or whether it is truly a gift from God when wisdom prevails, it's good to know God hears our prayers. He too values wisdom and wants us to develop wise practices, clear minds, and decidedly good hearts. Thank God today for the wisdom he has given you.

This world's wisdom is foolishness to God. —1 Corinthians 3:19

Lord, thank you for giving me a clear head and sound reasoning...

WEEK 10/ DAY 3: *For My Work*

I long to accomplish a great and noble task; but it is my chief duty to accomplish small tasks as if they were great and noble.
—Helen Keller

God has given you tremendous gifts to share and opportunities to grow. He knows what makes your heart sing and what strengthens your spirit. Whether you are doing big jobs that may be noticed by lots of people, or small jobs that may get no notice at all, do all your work to God's glory. He'll bless you every step of the way.

Whatever you do, do it from the heart for the Lord and not for people.
—Colossians 3:23

Lord, I am so grateful for my work. I'm grateful that you have found ways to use my talents for...

WEEK 10/ DAY 4: *For Life's Direction*

Take courage, and turn your troubles, which are without remedy,
into material for spiritual progress. Often turn to our Lord, who
is watching you, poor frail little being as you are, amid your labors
and distractions. —Francis de Sales

God pays attention to the details of your life. He sees you when you trudge slowly through the obstacles that keep you from your goals. He sees the amazing effort you make to stand and try again, to rise above the difficulties of life. He sees you and blesses you. You're never alone! God is with you always.

Be happy in your hope, stand your ground when you're in trouble, and devote your-
selves to prayer. —Romans 12:12

Lord, I confess that I sometimes lose my way. I'm so grateful to know you are always with me…

WEEK 10/ DAY 5: *For Strength and Courage*

Courage is the strength or choice to begin a change.
Determination is the persistence to continue in that change.
—Author unknown

Thank God for your backbone. That's right. You have more courage and inner strength than you may even recognize. You face life with incredible determination, trying new things, taking on new responsibilities, learning to go with the flow. Anytime you're overcome by physical or emotional or spiritual exhaustion, remember that you become stronger through Christ. Give him the thanks.

The LORD is my strength and my shield. / My heart trusts him. / I was helped, my
heart rejoiced, / and I thank him with my song. —Psalm 28:7

Lord, I thank you for the strength you give me to…

WEEK 10/ DAY 6: *For Good Neighbors*

The love of God is the first and great commandment. But love of our neighbor is the means by which we obey it. Since we cannot see God directly, God allows us to catch sight of him through our neighbor. By loving our neighbor we purge our eyes to see God. So love your neighbor and you will discover that in doing so you come to know God. —Augustine of Hippo

Whether your neighbors are simply a stone's throw from your driveway or a half mile down the road, or even the next town over, give God thanks for them. Neighbors celebrate the joys and sorrows of life with you. God truly had our best interest in mind when he commanded us to love our neighbors as ourselves.

Treat people in the same way that you want them to treat you. —Luke 6:31

Lord, thank you so much for my good neighbors, especially…

WEEK 10/ DAY 7: *For the World*

The early Christians did not say in dismay, "Look what the world has come to." Instead, with great delight they said, "Look Who has come into the world!" —Author unknown

We give thanks to our Creator for the world he has made and for the Son he delivered to bring us back to Himself. We give thanks that the world is a diverse, active, growing, changing, and challenging place and that God has set us in the midst of it all to make a difference.

I will give thanks to you, my Lord, among all the peoples;/ I will make music to you among the nations / because your faithful love is as high as heaven; / your faithfulness reaches the clouds. —Psalm 57:9-10

Lord, I thank you for this incredible world. Thank you for the part you have given me to play…

Thankful for Our Heroes

⟳

Pay the taxes you owe, pay the duties you are charged, give respect to those you should respect, and honor those you should honor.
—Romans 13:7

It's important to us to have heroes, role models, people we imagine we'd like to emulate. God knows our need for good examples and certainly in that light Jesus Christ is a hero, the one who truly came to save us from mortal danger.

Culturally though, we have heroes in our midst. We might think of those who serve us in the military, or police officers and firefighters who protect us. Certainly we're grateful when we call 911 and get an instant response to our dilemma. Yes, we have heroes all around us.

Others come to mind as well when we think of family members who have taught and guided us or teachers and preachers who have watched over our minds and spirits. We have physicians who guide us through our physical challenges and nurses who make sure we recover well.

The world is full of heroes. Some lead countries or cities or universities. Some protect our freedom or our rights as individuals. Some simply see us for who we are and challenge us to become more. They all fill our hearts with gratitude.

The most eloquent prayer is the prayer through hands that heal and bless. The highest form of worship is the worship of unselfish Christian service. The greatest form of praise is the sound of consecrated feet seeking out the lost and helpless. —Billy Graham

Lord, I thank you with all my heart for those who serve, who are heroes to us all...

WEEK 11 / DAY 2: *It's an Emergency!*

*No one was ever honored for what they received. Honor has been
the reward for what they gave.* —Calvin Coolidge

911! Those are the numbers we call when we're in the midst of a crisis. Someone has just been in an accident, someone needs an ambulance, or someone needs protection. How truly grateful we are for those who serve in this way, who make it possible for us to survive moments we could not handle all alone. Thank God for these heroes!

But the one who is greatest among you will be your servant. —Matthew 23:11

Lord, thank you for those who are on call to bring help when it's needed in any situation...

WEEK 11 / DAY 3: *Serving Around the World*

Only a life lived for others is worth living. —Albert Einstein

The men and women who serve America in the United States and in countries far and wide deserve our prayers and our gratitude for countless reasons. We are a nation that seeks individual freedom and truly desires peace for our brothers and sisters around the world. God has blessed us with the opportunity to serve him as prayer warriors for those who protect our freedom to worship and to live as we choose.

Live honorably among the unbelievers. —1 Peter 2:12

Lord, thank you for those who protect and defend us around the world. Our hearts are filled with gratitude for...

WEEK 11 / DAY 4: *More Than Politics and Politicians*

*The Lord doesn't ask about your ability, only your availability;
and, if you prove your dependability, the Lord will increase your
capability.* —Author unknown

Politics may strike an uncomfortable nerve, yet we cannot be too grateful that we live in a country with a system that encourages the freedom to believe, to speak, to strive, and to become whatever we might want to become. Politicians and political systems inspire us to dream of a better world and a better society.

And you have been filled by him, who is the head of every ruler and authority.
—Colossians 2:10

Lord, thank you for those men and women who choose to serve in the seat of government...

WEEK 11 / DAY 5: *Spreading the Word*

*The test of a preacher is that his congregation goes away saying,
not, "What a lovely sermon!" but, "I will do something."*
—Billy Graham

The men and women who have devoted themselves to the calling of God on their lives to be shepherds and guides to a diverse flock, inspire thanks. Their service goes beyond measure as they comfort the sick, grieve with the broken-hearted, and rejoice with those who celebrate. They share the Word, holding up the gospel in ways that challenge and protect our spirits. God bless them, every one!

And how can they hear without a preacher? And how can they preach unless they are sent? As it is written, How beautiful are the feet of those who announce the good news. —Romans 10:14-15

Lord, thank you so much for the people who have answered your call to tell others the good news of Jesus Christ...

WEEK 11 / DAY 6: *The School of Life*

The mediocre teacher tells. The good teacher explains. The superior teacher demonstrates. The great teacher inspires.
—William A. Ward

We've learned how to navigate the world by sometimes inspired and sometimes reluctant teachers. We've been blessed to grow and change and become and we owe a great deal of who we are to those who helped us understand our own value. Thank God for teachers, whose gifts are so numerous, they are truly without measure.

Train children in the way they should go; when they grow old, they won't depart from it. —Proverbs 22:6

Lord, thank you for giving us teachers who guide our way and challenge our thinking. Especially today, I thank you for…

WEEK 11 / DAY 7: *Leaders Make a Difference*

You must be careful how you walk, and where you go, for there are those following you who will set their feet where yours are set.
—Robert E. Lee

You know who they are! Leaders always stand out, always marching to a drummer that others may not hear. Leaders have the courage to challenge old ideas and start again to discover truth and opportunity. Leaders create a new path where none existed before. How grateful we are to those who help us move forward in every area of life.

Whoever wants to be great among you will be your servant. —Matthew 20:26

Lord, good leaders make a difference and those who serve you and lead others are worthy of our praise and thanks. Thank you for…

Thankful for Pets

❦

Give thanks to the LORD because he is good, / because his faithful love lasts forever!
—Psalm 107:1

Who can resist those innocent eyes, sparkling with joy simply because you came home? Sometimes, your best friends come on four feet and have a presence that is both charming and satisfying. Cats and dogs and other lovable pets are often the ones who remind you of your own humanity, who keep you humble and give you courage. It's safe to say that God helps us become our best selves with the gift of having a pet.

Pet owners certainly understand having a heart of gratitude for their precious friends and companions, who are furry and bright. This week, we'll give thanks for the pets who give us back a portion of ourselves through unfailing love. These are the ones who forgive us when we're wrong, demonstrate appreciation when we treat them well, and inspire our sense of peace when they rest comfortably nearby. Adorable, demanding, childlike, and courageous, there's nothing like a pet! Thank God for his kindness in providing us with such joy!

Until one has loved an animal, a part of one's soul remains unawakened.
—Anatole France

Lord, you have done so many incredible things for your children, and what joy it brings to have the love of a…

WEEK 12/ DAY 2: *Faithful to the End*

If having a soul means being able to feel love and loyalty and gratitude, then animals are better off than a lot of humans.
—James Herriot

If we struggle with the idea of what it means to be faithful to God, or to another person, perhaps we can take a look at those faithful and abiding pets who never question our motives, never criticize what we do, and always show up, ready to love and play again each time we come home. Pets are faithful to the end and unconditional in their love.

How awesome are your works, LORD! —Psalm 92:5

Lord, my little (pet's name) ____ is so faithful and loving to me. My heart fills with awe that he is mine! Thank you...

WEEK 12/ DAY 3: *Gentle Companions*

Animals are such agreeable friends—they ask no questions, they pass no criticisms. —George Eliot

When you sit and reflect, they sit and reflect beside you. When you run and play, they come quickly to join the fun. Whatever you're doing, it is a joy to their precious furry selves, to be right there, right beside you as companions and friends. God is good to have provided such incredible creatures to share the joys of life with us.

You who are righteous, / rejoice in the LORD and be glad! / All you whose hearts are right, sing out in joy! —Psalm 32:11

Lord, there is truly no one quite like you who would provide so well for our needs. Thank you so much for my faithful companion and pet...

WEEK 12/ DAY 4: *Just a Love Fest*

Love the animals: God has given them the rudiments of thought and joy untroubled. —Fyodor Dostoyevsky

Is there any better word than "love" to describe the way you feel about your pet? Certainly there are moments when they require something from you that feels like work, which feels demanding, but what love relationship doesn't require that? For the most part, your pet offers you tail-wagging, precious purring, gentle love, and it never fades away.

Live your life with love, following the example of Christ, who loved us and gave himself for us. —Ephesians 5:2

Lord, my pet is so lovable, so warm, and so friendly. I can't imagine what life would be like without him. Thank you...

⨌

WEEK 12/ DAY 5: *Some Furry Special Comforters!*

One reason a dog can be such a comfort when you're feeling blue is that he doesn't try to find out why. —Author unknown

Have you noticed the comforting feeling you get from simply sitting and rubbing your pet's fur? Sometimes, all you need and all your pet needs is a little time, a few moments of connection. God has blessed us with so many opportunities to feel his peace in our lives.

Peace I leave with you. My peace I give you. I give to you not as the world gives. Don't be troubled or afraid. —John 14:27

Lord, this little furry friend of mine brings me so much comfort. Thank you...

WEEK 12/ DAY 6: *Ambassadors of Good Will*

If all the beasts were gone, men would die from a great loneliness
of spirit, for whatever happens to the beasts also happens to the
man. All things are connected. Whatever befalls the Earth befalls
the sons of the Earth.
—Chief Seattle of the Suquamish Tribe

Pets are skilled at keeping loneliness from your day. They are ambassadors of good will, who guard your heart and mind, helping you understand how valuable and loved you really are. Thank God for his great wisdom and generosity in finding pets for unfulfilled hearts and homes.

Those who walk in innocence walk with confidence. —Proverbs 10:9

Lord, thank you for the companionship of my pet. Thanks again for…

❦

WEEK 12/ DAY 7: *Pets Come in All Shapes and Sizes*

Our perfect companions never have fewer than four feet.
—Colette

Whether your pet is bigger than you are or so small you have to watch where you walk in order to keep him safe, you are blessed. Your four-legged friend knows you and loves you just the way you are, keeps the light on for you when you're away, and leans in when life is difficult, offering you comfort and peace. Thanks be to God!

The people whose God is the LORD are truly happy! —Psalm 144:15

Lord, I am so happy to have my pet, _____. I thank you so much for…

Thankful for Change

∽◦◦◦∾

I have become all things to all people, so I could save some by all possible means.
—1 Corinthians 9:22

Talk about a chameleon!

All changes, even the most longed for, have their melancholy; for what we leave behind us is a part of ourselves; we must die to one life before we can enter another.
—Anatole France

Change is not only constant, it's sometimes dizzying. Things can move at such speed around you that you wonder how it happened. It's kind of like driving down a long stretch of road, mildly connected to what you're doing, but being so lost in thought that you get to your destination and realize you don't remember seeing anything along the way. It can be a somewhat scary realization. Change can happen that way too.

Sometimes you have change thrust upon you and other times you stir up the waters and cause it to come into being. Whether, like Paul, you change for every situation, hoping to bring others into your circle of influence, or whether you sit, doing your best to bar the door from change's unwelcome entry, it's a constant part of your life. In the next few days, give thanks for the somewhat uncomfortable, often unexpected, but absolutely essential thing in your life called change. It may offer you a new opportunity to understand your faith.

We must always change, renew, rejuvenate ourselves; otherwise we harden.
—Goethe

Lord, thank you for those things that cause me to desire changes in my life . . .

WEEK 13/ DAY 2: *A Bit of Reinvention*

Taking a new step, uttering a new word, is what people fear most.
—Fyodor Dostoevsky

Now and then, we're called upon to go right up to the mirror, take a good strong look, and make a decision to reinvent ourselves. If it's a conscious choice, we can seek prayerful guidance and consult with others who might advise us how to take the next steps. If it's an unconscious choice, we may simply have to ride the waves of change until we get comfortable again. Either way, God is leading the way and that's a reason to be grateful.

No one pours new wine into old leather wineskins; otherwise, the wine would burst the wineskins and the wine would be lost and the wineskins destroyed. But new wine is for new wineskins. —Mark 2:22

Lord, thank you for helping me reinvent myself, shedding the old me and embracing the new…

WEEK 13/ DAY 3: *Yesterday's Gone!*

Change is the law. And those who look only to the past or present are certain to miss the future. —John F. Kennedy

Yesterday has slipped away and you've risen to a brand new day. If you really consider how beautiful it is to witness and embrace the new you, it will surely make you smile. Things will change today because that's the way you grow. Give God the glory that he knows exactly what needs to change in your life.

Those who use the world should be like people who aren't preoccupied with it, because this world in its present form is passing away. —1 Corinthians 7:31

Lord, thank you for the things you are doing in my life to give me a brighter future…

WEEK 13/ DAY 4: *Keep on Growing!*

Don't ask for an easier life; ask to be a stronger person. Sometimes you just have to take the leap and build your wings on the way down. —Kobi Yamada

Thank God when you're truly interested in growing and becoming more of what God designed you to become. Those times offer the best opportunity to embrace change and to seek what might be next. There may well be times when you simply have to take a leap of faith. Thank God that he is always poised to catch you even in mid-flight.

Those who hope in the LORD / will renew their strength; / they will fly up on wings like eagles; / they will run and not be tired; / they will walk and not be weary. —Isaiah 40:31

Lord, thank you for showing me new things, new ways to grow…

WEEK 13/ DAY 5: *Why Should I Change?*

He who counts the stars and calls them by names, is in no danger of forgetting His own children. He knows your case as thoroughly as if you were the only creature He ever made, or the only saint He ever loved. —C. H. Spurgeon

God loves you too much to leave you the way you are. He walks with you every hour of your life, looking for ways to help you see him, to seek more of him, and to change your inner nature to reflect him. You are his personal concern. Thank him for his tremendous love for you.

But God shows his love for us, because while we were still sinners Christ died for us. —Romans 5:8

Lord, thank you for loving me so much that you prompt me to change…

WEEK 13/ DAY 6: *Never Too Late to Change*

Be thankful for this day, bringing new insights, strengthening your thoughts and reminding you of how much more there is that you've yet to discover. Today is a good day to change your thoughts for the better. —Karen Moore

Sometimes we resist change, giving ourselves excuses that make us feel more comfortable, at least temporarily. We reason that we're too old, or we're okay the way we are, or others are to blame for our not being what we might have been. We lie to ourselves. Thank God today for those moments when you embrace all that he has for you and make a joyful change.

My plans aren't your plans, / nor are your ways my ways, says the LORD. —Isaiah 55:8

Lord, thank you for all the effort you put into moving me forward, to keep me from making mind-numbing excuses for not changing…

WEEK 13/ DAY 7: *Fear of Change*

We gain strength, and courage, and confidence by each experience in which we really stop to look fear in the face. … We must do that which we think we cannot. —Eleanor Roosevelt

You can do it! You can overcome your fears to grow and change. You have a powerful spirit within you that God gave you on the day you were born and it wants you to try and try again. God has graciously provided you with all the tools you need for successful outcomes. Give him the praise!

God didn't give us a spirit that is timid but one that is powerful, loving, and self-controlled. —2 Timothy 1:7

Lord, thank you for giving me a strong spirit…

Thankful for Positive Spirit

Anxiety is the rust of life, destroying its brightness and weakening its power. A childlike and abiding trust in Providence is its best preventive and remedy.
—*Author unknown*

The way you look at life, the way you handle the good and the bad and the ugly, makes all the difference. If you and your best friend have the exact same life, but one of you embraces the ups and downs and sees the good in all that happens and one of you is sure that the bottom will fall out no matter what happens, you will each experience totally different lives. Any time you manage to keep a positive spirit and an attitude of joy and expectancy, you defeat the enemy because you live better.

Your positive attitude tells the world that you may not know all about tomorrow or what may happen, but you totally understand that the tomorrows are always in God's hand and you put all your trust in him. One of your greatest attributes and lasting treasures will be your attitude of joy. Thank God for this incredible gift.

Don't be troubled. Trust in God. Trust also in me. —Jesus, in John 14:1

Lord, I thank you for giving me an attitude of joy, one that is buoyant and able to move through life's ups and downs…

WEEK 14/ DAY 2: *What Do You Expect?*

We block Christ's advance in our lives by failure of expectation.
Of course this is just one form of lack of faith. But it is so purely
negative that it escapes detection. —William Temple

Are you expecting good things to happen to you today? Are you ready to receive all that God has planned for you? It's not always easy, but it's a good practice to simply start the day, thanking God for all the possibilities and all the good things you believe he wants to bring your way. It sets your heart on a path of joy.

All things are possible for God. —Matthew 19:26

Lord, thank you that I can trust you and expect good things…

WEEK 14/ DAY 3: *Seeing the Good in Others*

We ought to do good to others as simply and as naturally as a
horse runs, or a bee makes honey, or a vine bears grapes season
after season without thinking of the grapes it has borne.
—Marcus Aurelius

It's a great day to be thankful for those people you know who continually do good for others. It doesn't seem to matter if they get thanked in return, get recognized for their kindness, or get nothing at all. They simply do good things because it is natural for them to do so. Count yourself blessed when you have people like that in your life.

Don't forget to do good and to share what you have because God is pleased with
these kinds of sacrifices. —Hebrews 13:16

Lord, I am truly blessed to have good people in my life…

WEEK 14/ DAY 4: *The Sun Will Come Out Tomorrow*

*Got no checkbooks, got no banks, / Still I'd like to express my
thanks—/ I got the sun in the morning and the moon at night.*
—Irving Berlin, "I Got the Sun in the Morning"

Whether it's raining today or not, it's best to bring your own sunshine wherever you go. That sunshine is always within you in the form of God's Spirit and the light he gives you to bring you joy. Give God a shout out today for that special sunshine which will radiate in your life tomorrow after tomorrow.

Renew the thinking in your mind by the Spirit and clothe yourself with the new person created according to God's image in justice and true holiness. —Ephesians 4:23-24

Lord, thank you for infusing me with a positive spirit, fully believing and trusting in your goodness…

WEEK 14/ DAY 5: *Giving Thanks in All Circumstances*

*Life is a hard fight, a struggle, a wrestling with the principle of evil,
hand to hand, foot to foot. The night is given us to take breath, to
pray, to drink deep at the fountain of power. The day causes us to
use the strength which has been given us, to go forth to work with
it till the evening.* —Florence Nightingale

It isn't always easy to maintain a positive attitude when your circumstances seem desperate and your prayers continue to go unanswered. It is then that you simply must take the time to stop, breathe in the mercy and grace of heaven, and find reason to be grateful in spite of the circumstances. God's light will shine through.

Give thanks in every situation because this is God's will for you in Christ Jesus. Don't suppress the Spirit. —1 Thessalonians 5:18-19

Lord, though I don't always understand the events surrounding my life, I thank you…

WEEK 14/ DAY 6: *Stay Calm and Keep Moving On*

With malice toward none; with charity for all; with firmness in the right, as God gives us to see the right…let us strive on to finish the work we are in. —Abraham Lincoln

When you rose with the morning sun, you were guaranteed one thing. For you, the work continues. For you, God has great plans as long as you continue to strive, continue to believe, and make an effort to do what you've been called to do today. Thank God today that he has called you to do a good work.

Let's not get tired of doing good, because in time we'll have a harvest if we don't give up. —Galatians 6:9

Lord, in the best of times and in the worst of times, I give you thanks for the work I do…

WEEK 14/ DAY 7: *Poised for Greatness*

God has entrusted me with myself. —Epictetus

Since God knows everything about you, he knew all along that you would come to this day. You are poised for greatness because he has put a bit of himself within you, giving you a positive spirit for growth and change and responsibility. You are the work of his hands, and so it is good to praise him for all he is now doing and will yet do in your life.

The attitude that comes from the Spirit leads to life and peace. —Romans 8:6

Lord, I thank you for impressing me with a sense of mission and a spirit of joy ready to move forward…

Thankful for What I've Learned

≈

The wise hear them and grow in wisdom; those with understanding gain guidance.
—*Proverbs 1:5*

Certainly we hope to be among the wise, those who gain insight from the things we experience and are taught. We hope that with each experience we take away the good news, the lesson that will benefit us as we continue life's journey. Sometimes we learn "the hard way," meaning we probably weren't listening the first time the opportunity came our way. Other times, we surprise ourselves with the brilliant grasp we seem to have about an event or concept. We grow instantly and mature ever so slightly.

Teachers come to us throughout our lives in many forms. Some helped us achieve standards of excellence so we could go on for further discipline and achievement. Some helped us see the value in a situation that seemed useless to our minds. The gift of life is that each experience becomes a teacher, and whether or not we appreciate the lesson has a lot to do with how much we embrace the good that comes.

Give God thanks and praise for all you are learning today.

Anyone who stops learning is old, whether twenty or eighty. Anyone who keeps learning stays young. The greatest thing in life is to keep your mind young.
—Henry Ford

Lord, I am truly grateful for the gift of learning…

WEEK 15/ DAY 2: *Learning from Mistakes*

If you don't learn from your mistakes, there's no sense making them. —Author unknown

It may seem like a strange idea to offer God thanks for those disasters in your life that you hate to even think about. Perhaps you'd like to sweep pieces of your life mosaic under the rug and hope no one ever reminds you of them. The fact is that many of those magnificent blunders helped shape you into the marvelous person you are today.

The secret things belong to the LORD our God. The revealed things belong to us and to our children forever. —Deuteronomy 29:29

Lord, you know my list of mistakes isn't exactly short. Even so, I thank you for each of them and for what I've learned...

WEEK 15/ DAY 3: *Roots and Wings*

Every effort to make society sensitive to the importance of the family is a great service to humanity. —Pope John Paul II

The nuclear family is the center of learning, the place where you learned to experience some bumps without getting bruised, a place to prepare you for a world that is not always forgiving or operating on the love of Christ. You're rooted in your heritage and so it is wise to give thanks to the ones who provided you with both the roots and the wings.

Those who trouble their family will inherit the wind. —Proverbs 11:29

Lord, I thank you for all that I learned from my family, as imperfect as it might be...

WEEK 15/ DAY 4: *Souls and Spirits*

The teacher, if he is indeed wise, does not bid you to enter the house of this wisdom but leads you to the threshold of your own mind. —Kahlil Gibran

We are thankful for those teachers who have caused us to think, to explore, to take something we didn't know before and digest it fully. They may have been teachers at home or at school or at church, but they were graciously put in our path, to ensure a successful life. Thank God, they have taught us well.

Get wisdom; get understanding. Don't forget and don't turn away from my words. —Proverbs 4:5

Lord, your teachers have influenced my life and helped me become the person I am, and I am grateful for each of them...

WEEK 15/ DAY 5: *Grateful for Church*

The church is the gathering of God's children, where they can be helped and fed like babies and then, guided by her motherly care, grow up to manhood in maturity of faith. —John Calvin

Your experience with the body of Christ, those you gather with for worship and praise, is God's provision for your spirit and your soul. It's the place where you can shake off the dust of uncertainty and stand firm in your belief. It's the place where you can absorb as much as your spirit and mind are willing to grasp. Praise God!

God's purpose is now to show the rulers and powers in the heavens the many different varieties of his wisdom through the church. —Ephesians 3:10

Lord, I thank you that I live in a country where I can attend church and worship you and learn...

WEEK 15/ DAY 6: *Friends and Enemies*

In Jesus and for him, enemies and friends alike are to be loved.
—Thomas à Kempis

You've learned untold lessons from those who surround you, the ones who love you always and the ones who would turn the other way at your approach. They each have something gracious and worthy to teach you. The lesson may be one of forgiveness or forbearance, or it may be one of finding peace and letting go. Thank God as you marvel at all he has done in your personal relationships.

Love your enemies, do good, and lend expecting nothing in return. —Luke 6:35

Lord, you have certainly taught me great lessons through those who did not understand me or who merely caused my heart to weep. I pray for those people and thank you for…

WEEK 15/ DAY 7: *Life Lessons 101*

The unexamined life is not worth living. —Socrates

Each time you pause to take stock of your life, the highs and lows, the moments of brilliance and passion, sometimes followed by weeks of uncertainty and unrest, causes you to learn. Life is its own kind of school and you will always be one of its brightest and best students as long as you seek the guidance of the One who created you. Thank him and praise him today.

I came so that they could have life—indeed, so that they could live life to the fullest. —John 10:10

Lord, I thank you for my life and the things I have learned so far…

Thankful for Gifts of Joy

Let all who take refuge in you celebrate. / Let them sing out loud forever! / Protect them so that all who love your name / can rejoice in you.
—Psalm 5:11

What brings you joy? What happens that causes you to realize you're happy, joyful, and genuinely delighted with the world around you? It may not always be something you're aware of. In fact, we live in a culture that talks a lot more about depression than we do about joy. We get used to the idea that many people live in a perpetual state of unhappiness.

God does not want that for you! He wants you to know that he loves you so much that he is practically giddy with delight. He thinks you're some of his best work and so he wants you to celebrate the relationship that the two of you share. Celebrate and then seek those moments of joy that he prepares just to see you smile. He wants you to radiate with love and blessing.

All those simple joys add up to one grateful heart. Share your grateful heart with him this week.

Christ is not only a remedy for your weariness and trouble, but he will give you an abundance of the contrary, joy and delight. —Jonathan Edwards

For those simple joys of life, I thank you, Father, especially for…

WEEK 16/ DAY 2: *Latté Moments*

Joy is everywhere. —Author Unknown

Those stand-alone coffee emporiums that grace the cities and towns of America bring people together and provide a comforting space for old friends, business friends, or those simply seeking a few quiet moments for themselves. There's nothing quite like the simple joy that allows you to stop everything, sip a savory delight, and contemplate a world of possibilities. Thank God for simple joys.

A happy heart has a continual feast. —Proverbs 15:15

Lord, thank you for the little joy-breaks you give me…

WEEK 16/ DAY 3: *To Market, to Market*

The odds of going to the store for a loaf of bread and coming out with only a loaf of bread are three billion to one.
—Erma Bombeck

The grocery store is an explosion of products and treasures. It's no longer a place where you run in and pick up a loaf of bread or a jug of milk. It's a showcase of American culture, a goldmine of opportunities to explore. It caters to your every whim, from creating a dining masterpiece to changing a light bulb. It's a veritable wonderland and offers instant joy to your life.

Better a meal of greens with love than a plump calf with hate. —Proverbs 15:17

Lord, I don't always think of going to the grocery store as a joyful event, but I have to admit it makes life easier so thank you…

WEEK 16/ DAY 4: *Good Job!*

Thou shalt ever joy at eventide if you spend the day fruitfully.
—Thomas à Kempis

There's nothing like a job well done to give you a sense of achievement and some much deserved joy. When others recognize your work, it's an even greater cause for celebration for it's gratifying to be appreciated for something you've worked hard to accomplish. Thank God for the people who bring great joy simply by noting you've done something extremely well.

I have fought the good fight, finished the race, and kept the faith. —2 Timothy 4:7

Lord, thank you for the joy that comes from doing a job well…

WEEK 16/ DAY 5: *Joy to the World!*

You must keep all earthly treasures out of your heart, and let Christ be your treasure, and let him have your heart.
—C. H. Spurgeon

Each Christmas we sing a rousing chorus of "Joy to the World!" We're reminded somewhere deep within our souls that joy comes through the heart, and when our hearts are linked to Jesus and his love we truly do have joy. We thank Christ our Lord for joy beyond measure, our treasure for always.

Where your treasure is, there your heart will be also. —Matthew 6:21

Lord, thank you for the joy that comes from my relationship with you…

WEEK 16/ DAY 6: *A Touch of Beauty!*

Beauty is the gift of God. —Aristotle

Have you ever stopped to truly thank God for all that is beautiful in the world? From mountain ranges to glimmering lakes and streams, to rain forests and beaches, we're blessed with beauty. Today, as you consider a fading sunset or the gleam in your child's eye, thank God for the amazing touches of beauty in your life.

Notice how the lilies in the field grow. They don't wear themselves out with work, and they don't spin cloth. But I say to you that even Solomon in all of his splendor wasn't dressed like one of these. —Matthew 6:28-29

Lord, the visions of beautiful things from landscapes to artwork to people I love show me what is beautiful, and I thank you…

WEEK 16/ DAY 7: *The Joy of a New Relationship*

Appreciation is a wonderful thing; it makes what is excellent in others belong to us as well. —Voltaire

Whenever you embark on a new relationship, whether it's romantic or in business or in friendship, there's a spark of joy that exists. It's new and it feels exciting and full of hope and possibility. Those moments of joy are gifts to our lives and worthy of praise.

Yes, goodness and faithful love will pursue me all the days of my life. —Psalm 23:6

Lord, thank you for that spirit of joy that permeates new relationships and experiences…

Thankful for the Right Work

We are God's coworkers, and you are God's field, God's building.
—*1 Corinthians 3:9*

You spent a number of years preparing yourself for the work you do today. You went to college or you got specific training and experience. You did it because you had a dream or a passion for the direction of your life and goals you wanted to meet. When you discover that you're actually doing your "right work" or the thing you feel divinely guided to do, it's an awesome thing. In fact, it's nearly everything because you then have a chance to truly be a coworker with God out in his field.

If you're not yet set in that work, then look with gratitude at all you are experiencing, because each aspect of it will enable you to embrace the right opportunity when it shows itself. In the meantime, do all that you do knowing that you serve a living God who sees you right where you are.

Thank God—every morning when you get up—that you have something to do which must be done, whether you like it or not. Being forced to work and forced to do your best, will breed in you a hundred virtues which the idle never know.
—Charles Kingsley

Lord, thank you for giving me opportunities to work for you…

WEEK 17/ DAY 2: *Working for Myself*

God helps them that help themselves. —Benjamin Franklin

You may be self-employed or you may go to a place of business each day, but either way, you work for yourself. You work to make a difference. You work to honor your family and God. You work because it's the right thing for you to do. Thank God that he blesses the work of your hands.

Then people go off to their work, to do their work until evening. —Psalm 104:23

Lord, thank you so much for the work you've given me to do…

WEEK 17/ DAY 3: *Working for Others*

Every successful business in the world is in existence because its founder recognized in a problem or need an opportunity to be of service to others. Every problem or need in your life is in reality an opportunity to call forth inner resources of wisdom, love, strength, and ability. —J. Sig Paulson

Whether you're making the beds to keep your home clean and bright for your family, or creating another report for your boss, your work is an opportunity to share your significant resources, all designed for the good of others. God has called you to do great work for him.

Get to work. Don't be afraid or discouraged, because the LORD God, my God, is with you. —1 Chronicles 28:20

Lord, I do thank you for the opportunity to work…

WEEK 17/ DAY 4: *The Right Job for Me*

Always keep your eyes open for the little task, because it is the little task that is important to Jesus Christ. The future of the kingdom of God does not depend on the enthusiasm of this or that powerful person; those great ones are necessary too, but it is equally necessary to have a great number of little people who will do a little thing in the service of Christ. —Albert Schweitzer

God wants you to be fulfilled, overflowing with a sense of joy in the work you do. The work you do for him is always the "right" work, and he knows how to help you share your gifts and talents in ways that please both of you. He loves to see you happy in your work.

Stand firm, unshakable, excelling in the work of the Lord as always, because you know that your labor isn't going to be for nothing in the Lord. —1 Corinthians 15:58

Lord, your love for me is awesome, and I thank you for the work I'm privileged to do…

WEEK 17/ DAY 5: *The Freedom to Choose*

You will find, as you look back upon your life, that the moments that stand out are the moments when you have done things for others. —Henry Drummond

Imagine what it would be like if you could not choose the work you do, if someone told you what you would do and where you would do it, regardless of your desires or talents or abilities. Thank God you live in a place that gives you the opportunity to serve and become all that you desire.

If you are actually able to be free, take advantage of the opportunity. —1 Corinthians 7:21

Lord, thank you that I am so blessed in my work…

WEEK 17/ DAY 6: *Opening New Doors*

When one door closes another door opens; but we so often look so long and so regretfully upon the closed door, that we do not see the ones which open for us. —Alexander Graham Bell

Thank God for closed doors. Thank him that you have an opportunity to grow and become more each time you find it necessary to seek his guidance again for your life and your work. He has more opportunities for you than you will ever have time to take to full advantage.

My life is stuck in the dirt. Now make me live again according to your promise! —Psalm 119:25

Lord, thank you for not leaving me in places that no longer serve me or you or cause me to feel stuck…

WEEK 17/ DAY 7: *Success and Failure*

There are a lot of ways to become a failure, but never taking a chance is the most successful. —Author unknown

Sometimes the work we do leaves us feeling like we're stuck in a rut, with no way to advance to a better opportunity and nowhere to go. We wonder if we're even doing the right thing anymore because we have no passion for it and everything we once liked about it has drained away our energy and spirit. God sees you right where you are and is eager to give you new hope and opportunities.

Commit your work to the Lord, and your plans will succeed. —Proverbs 16:3

Lord, as always, I am overcome with your goodness to me, your willingness to keep guiding me to do the work you want me to do…

Thankful for Creation

Everything came into being through the Word, / and without the Word / nothing came into being.
—John 1:3

Isn't it thrilling to take a trip to a place you've never seen? Maybe you travel to a rich and diverse rain forest and explore the lush vegetation. You might feel like you've just set foot in the Garden of Eden. Maybe you stand on a mountain top and survey the incredible sense of peace from the valley below. Maybe you're simply taking in the beauty of a field of buttercups and daisies. Whatever it is, you can't help feeling the awe and the presence of God.

Imagine the Creator spinning the intricate webs of hundreds of varieties of spiders, each one beautiful in its design and purpose. Imagine him reveling in the fishes of the sea with their vibrant, watery colors and shapes and sizes. Imagine again what he must have been thinking when he determined the sizes and shapes and colors of human beings. We have a Creator who lavished us with rich variety, never seeking the monotony of sameness, never demanding that each one look just like the one before it as though he only used a great cookie cutter to get his work done. Imagination stirred our Creator to awesome possibility, to things we have yet to discover. Thank God we have a rich and beautiful universe.

There is about us, if only we have eyes to see, a creation of such spectacular profusion, spendthrift richness, and absurd detail, as to make us catch our breath in astonished wonder. —Michael Mayne

Lord, we're in awe of all that you have done, all you've created to give us a rich existence…

WEEK 18/ DAY 2: *Animal Instincts*

Kindness to all God's creatures is an absolute rock-bottom necessity if peace and righteousness are to prevail.
—Sir Wilfred Grenfell

How awesome it is to have aquariums full of brightly colored fishes, and oceans full of such diverse creatures we can hardly take it in. If you're a cat lover or a dog enthusiast, it's hard not to get caught up in each unique animal from the tips of their furry heads to their cute little paws. The long and the short tail of it—that is, tale of it—is that God has blessed us with an array of wonderful animals to observe, to respect, and to love with all our hearts. Thank him today for that gift.

When you happen to come upon your enemy's ox or donkey that has wandered off, you should bring it back to them. —Exodus 23:4

Lord, you've taught us from ancient days to take care of the animals on our planet, and so we thank you for them…

WEEK 18/ DAY 3: *Every Day Is Earth Day!*

Take care of the earth and she will take care of you.
—Author unknown

We know that we are blessed indeed to have beautiful mountains' majesty, oceans teeming with life, and forests rich in diversity. We are the recipients of all our Creator has done to give us life. Life is everywhere sacred and holy. Thank God for his incredible goodness.

The earth is the LORD's / and everything in it, / the world and its inhabitants too.
—Psalm 24:1

Lord , thank you for creating such incredible landscapes for us to enjoy…

WEEK 18/ DAY 4: *Of Daffodils and Violets*

Flowers are the sweetest things God ever made, and forgot to put a soul into. —Henry Beecher

A red rose may mean love from one person to another, but God shows how incredible his love for us really is in the amazing diversity of all he set to bloom. Flowers attend us at celebrations of marriage, of life, and of death. They offer forgiveness and simple kindness. How grateful we are for every bit of joy and beauty we receive from flowers.

Blossoms have appeared in the land; / the season of singing has arrived / and the sound of the turtledove is heard in our land. —Song of Songs 2:12

For the precious beauty of flowers, for the joy they bring in such an unassuming way, I thank you, Lord…

WEEK 18/ DAY 5: *Of Humble Humanity*

We cannot live only for ourselves. A thousand fibers connect us with our fellow men! —Herman Melville

As human beings, created by God in his image, we cannot help feeling the connection between us, regardless of where we inhabit the planet or what color our skin may have turned out to be. We are hearts and minds and spirits blessed by our Creator. How wonderful that he gave us such strength in our diversity to become his hands and feet all over the globe.

If possible, to the best of your ability, live at peace with all people. —Romans 12:18

Lord, thank you for my brothers and sisters everywhere, all over the planet, for you are the Father of us all…

WEEK 18/ DAY 6: *Colors of Joy*

Why do two colors, put one next to the other, sing? Can one really explain this? No. —Pablo Picasso

Only God knew what colors would magnify his work with such splendor. He could have made the skies pink instead of comforting and peaceful blue. He could have made water orange instead of clear and pure and available for so many other possibilities. From your first box of crayons to the color palette of your dreams, give God credit for his imaginative use of color.

If any of you are happy, they should sing. —James 5:13

Lord, surely I would sing to you today in thanksgiving for your gift of colors, giving us breathtaking panoramas and untold joys in life…

WEEK 18/ DAY 7: *For Every Season*

If we had no winter, the spring would not be so pleasant; if we did not sometimes taste of adversity, prosperity would not be so welcome. —Anne Bradstreet

We may not always clap our hands at the changing seasons of life, winter's chill or springtime rains, and yet, there's something so gratifying, so soul-fulfilling in these simple events caused by an ever turning globe, that we must give thanks again to the One who made it so. God bless every season of the year, as well as the seasons of our lives.

There's a season for everything and a time for every matter under the heavens. —Ecclesiastes 3:1

Lord, thank you for the richness of each season for all your creation…

Thankful for Worship

⁂

Declare God's glory among the nations; / declare his wondrous works among all people / because the LORD is great and so worthy of praise.

—*1 Chronicles 16:24-25*

You may find your heart ready to worship nearly any place you go. You may want to sing out praise and glory to God when you have a moment to sit quietly by a mountain stream, or stand at the peak of a mountain ridge in great wonder. You may seek to praise him on a Sunday morning when your heart has been stirred by the beauty of the choir's song or the pastor's sermon.

Worship is a state of being because it comes from the heart flowing outward, recognizing our humanness and God's greatness. When you have the opportunity through prayer or quiet moments, or singing at the top of your lungs driving in your car, you continue to worship. What grace and glory and joy beyond measure is given to our spirits any time we experience the grandeur of worshipping our heavenly Father. Praise his name!

The Glory of God, and, as our only means to glorifying Him, the salvation of human souls, is the real business of life. —C. S. Lewis

Lord, it is with joy and thanksgiving that I come to worship you today…

WEEK 19/ DAY 2: *In Praise and Adoration*

When we wake up each morning, if praise of the risen Christ were to fill our hearts…then in the monotony of daily life, an inner surge of vitality would reveal our hidden longing.
—Brother Roger

You have a chance to wake up with Jesus today. You can open your eyes to the world and even before you scurry out of bed to head out for the day, you can behold him. You can thank him for all that you are and all that your life is about because of his great love for you. He is so worthy of your praise and gratitude.

Stand up and bless the LORD your God. / From everlasting to everlasting bless your glorious name, / which is high above all blessing and praise. —Nehemiah 9:5

Lord, for your bountiful blessings beyond anything I can measure, I thank you…

WEEK 19/ DAY 3: *Free to Worship*

I was not born to be free. I was born to adore and obey.
—C. S. Lewis

The founding fathers of America thought the freedom to worship God however we chose was so important, they fought wars and died to protect that right. Ever since, soldiers have fought for the freedom we prize so much today. Thank God that we are free to worship or not worship him as we choose.

Sing to the LORD, / who has done glorious things; / proclaim this throughout all the earth. —Isaiah 12:5

Lord, thank you that I can so freely lift my arms in praise for your goodness and kindness to me…

WEEK 19/ DAY 4: *Dance and Sing!*

Let us sing how the eternal God, the author of all marvels, first
created the heavens for the sons of men as a roof to cover them,
and how their almighty Protector gave them the earth to live in.
—Caedmon

Praise him for the earth, the planet teeming with life that provides you with every possible thing you need to grow. Give him thanks that he has in every way created opportunities for your heart, mind, and spirit to know him better. Dance and sing! It will do your heart good.

Let them praise God's name with dance; let them sing God's praise with the drum and lyre! —Psalm 149:3

Thank you, dear Lord, for your creation, the earth that supports my life and the heaven that brings you glory…

WEEK 19/ DAY 5: *Everybody Praise!*

Praising God is one of the highest and purest acts of religion. In
prayer we act like men; in praise we act like angels.
—Thomas Watson

Something significant, nearly miraculous, happens when we turn our hearts from honest prayers to humble praise. We are free to go to the throne any time we need help or we need to simply rest in God's care. Better yet, though, are those moments when we are wholly given over to heartfelt thanks and praise.

Sing to the LORD a new song; / sing God's praise in the assembly of the faithful!
—Psalm 149:1

Lord, I praise you with all my heart…

WEEK 19/ DAY 6: *In the Gift of Communion*

When the remembrance of God lives in the heart and there maintains the fear of Him, then all goes well; but when this remembrance grows weak or is kept only in the head, then all goes astray.
—Theophan the Recluse

We celebrate the death and resurrection of our Lord and Savior each time we have the opportunity to take communion. We bind our hearts and our souls to his, seeking to draw ever closer to all that he is. Let us give thanks each time we so consciously draw near to him, for he comes quickly to embrace us.

I received a tradition from the Lord, which I also handed on to you: on the night on which he was betrayed, the Lord Jesus took bread. After giving thanks, he broke it and said, "This is my body, which is for you; do this to remember me."
—1 Corinthians 11:23-24

Lord, thank you for giving us such a wonderful way to remember you…

WEEK 19/ DAY 7: *In the Still Moments*

Silence is the mother of prayer. It frees the prisoner; it guards the divine flame; it watches over reasoning; it protects the sense of penitence. —John Climacus

We sometimes shy away from those quiet spaces, fearful perhaps of hearing too much of our voice. As we begin to quiet the noise of daily life, the stillness welcomes the voice of the One who desires nothing more than to sit with us and give us his peace. Thank God for those sweet, still moments.

In return and rest you will be saved; / quietness and trust will be your strength.
—Isaiah 30:15

O, Lord, how I long for those moments to sit quietly and worship you…

Thankful for Simple Pleasures

*Go, eat your food joyfully and drink your wine happily because
God has already accepted what you do.*
—Ecclesiastes 9:7

God knows you and accepts you just as you are. He invites you to come to his table. He encourages you to share your heart and your prayers and he celebrates with you when life brings you happy moments.

You're so special to God, he wants you to enjoy the simple things that will make you smile. If indulging in a piece of strawberry cheesecake makes you happy, he's happy. If going through the scrapbook of your life and recalling people and occasions that brought you joy uplifts your heart, he's delighted. Whatever makes you happy, whatever simple pleasures give you rest from the harder things of life, those are the things your loving Father wants for you. Imagine his excitement each time he knows something wonderful is about to happen to you. Imagine how much it means to him to provide you with exactly what you need at just the right time. You're loved, and one of the best ways God can show you how much is through indulging you, offering you some quiet and simple pleasures. Let your heart thank him for those things.

Our mind is where our pleasure is, our heart is where our treasure is, our love is where our life is, but all these, our pleasure, treasure, and life, are reposed in Jesus Christ.
—Thomas Adams

Lord, I love how you give me so many little moments to enjoy…

WEEK 20/ DAY 2: *Play Time*

The real joy of life is in its play. Play is anything we do for the joy and love of doing it, apart from any profit, compulsion, or sense of duty. It is the real living of life with the feeling of freedom and self-expression. —Walter Rauschenbusch

Did you ever notice how much better life feels when you've managed to get away, even for a few minutes, to let your mind play freely with an idea, or stop at lunchtime and shoot a few hoops? Somehow life is just better. God knows you need time to let your hair down.

I know that there's nothing better for them but to enjoy themselves and do what's good while they live. —Ecclesiastes 3:12

Lord, thanks for knowing I need a little play time, time that's just refreshing to my spirit...

WEEK 20/ DAY 3: *Dinner for Two*

Life is a combination of magic and pasta. —Federico Fellini

One of the simple pleasures of life is creating a lovely meal just for two, something special for you and one other person. The whole process engages the intellect, the culinary skill, and the heart. How grateful we are when we can take the time to create, to dine with someone we love, and to enjoy the moment. Thank God!

This is the gift of God: that all people should eat, drink, and enjoy the results of their hard work. —Ecclesiastes 3:13

Lord, it's been a while since I busied myself with making a truly special meal, so thank you for the moments when I do...

WEEK 20/ DAY 4: *For the Love of a Book*

Everywhere I have sought rest and not found it, except sitting in a corner by myself with a little book. —Thomas à Kempis

There's something almost magical about a new book. You appreciate the cover design, the smell of the paper and the inks, the format and design. You put the book away, anticipating the moment when you'll be drawn into it, savoring the words while you sip a bit of tea. It's pure pleasure. Give God the glory!

Pay attention to public reading, preaching, and teaching. —1 Timothy 4:13

Lord, I love the quiet moments when I have a chance to settle back and read…

WEEK 20/ DAY 5: *Reasons to Smile*

Always laugh when you can; it is cheap medicine. Merriment is a philosophy not well understood. It is the sunny side of existence. —Lord Byron

Finding a reason to smile or causing someone else to smile brings joy to the heart. Thank God for those divine moments when you can simply laugh at yourself, at life, or at the situation in which you find yourself. It's good to take a walk on the sunny side of life.

There's a season for everything and a time for every matter under the heavens:… a time for crying and a time for laughing. —Ecclesiastes 3:1, 4

Lord, thank you for giving us a sense of humor, the ability to laugh and enjoy the moment…

WEEK 20/ DAY 6: *Sunshine on a Cloudy Day*

It's a beautiful world to see, / Or it's all choked up and gray, / For whether it shines or rains a lot / Only your heart can say.
—Karen Moore

When you're in love, or you're happy with life, everything makes you smile. Rainy days are more relaxing, and sunny days invite you to play. Thank God when you have an attitude of joy and peace.

Be glad in the Lord always! Again I say, be glad! —Philippians 4:4

Lord, I thank you for each day when I arise to new opportunities regardless of sunshine or rain…

WEEK 20/ DAY 7: *Singing a Happy Tune!*

God respects me when I work, but he loves me when I sing.
—Tagore

Sometimes you just have a simple song that goes in and out of your head. Sometimes you can't help singing at the top of your lungs in your car or the privacy of your shower. Whenever a little song comes from your heart, it's pure joy to God's ears.

The LORD is my strength and my shield./ My heart trusts him. / I was helped, my heart rejoiced, and I thank him with my song. —Psalm 28:7

Lord, I thank you for the songs that lift my heart and cause me to rejoice…

Thankful for Freedom

Christ has set us free for freedom. Therefore stand firm and don't submit to the bondage of slavery again.
—Galatians 5:1

Celebrate freedom this week! In Christ, you are free to meet life differently than those who don't acknowledge him. You have the freedom to bow before your heavenly King and lay your sorrows and your joys at his feet. You have the freedom to explore new territories, try new things, gain new perspective in ways that serve him and others better.

The freedom to worship as you want, to praise him freely wherever you are, to become the person God designed you to be...those are freedoms worthy of everlasting thanks. You are his work and his design, and he set you free on planet earth to grow in him and know him.

Free to love, free to live, free to make mistakes and free to be forgiven, free to give heartfelt thanks...what gifts God has given you!

Set me free from evil passions, and heal my heart of all inordinate affections; that being inwardly cured and thoroughly cleansed, I may be made fit to love, courageous to suffer, steady to persevere. —Thomas à Kempis

Lord, I am so grateful for the many ways I experience a sense of freedom in my life...

WEEK 21 / DAY 2: *Life, Liberty, and the Pursuit of Happiness*

I asked God for all things, that I might enjoy life. God gave life,
that I might enjoy all things. —Author unknown

What incredible freedom we have to pursue our dreams! We can go to school, get training, run our own business, do whatever we want. We are blessed with the options and the opportunities because of God's faithful love and desire to have us become what God designed us to be. Thanks be to God!

Your faithful love is priceless, God! / Humanity finds refuge in the shadow of your wings. / They feast on the bounty of your house; / you let them drink from your river of pure joy. / Within you is the spring of life. / In your light, we see light. —Psalm 36:7-9

Lord, it brings me tears of joy to know that your faithfulness is not dependent on my doing everything right. You see me and my efforts and you help me become a better person. Thank you so much!

WEEK 21 / DAY 3: *Do What You Love*

We make a living by what we get. We make a life by what we give.
—Martin Luther King, Jr.

You're free to go to work today. You've been blessed with a talent, a special gift from God to make your life happier and more rewarding. You have something to give that no one else has. God has his fingerprint on your life and your design. How marvelous are his works!

Enjoy the LORD, / and he will give what your heart asks. / Commit your way to the LORD! / Trust him! He will act / and will make your righteousness shine like the dawn.
—Psalm 37:4-6

Lord, I am truly grateful for the work of my hands, the work you gave me to do...

WEEK 21 / DAY 4: *See the World!*

We travel to learn; I have never been in any country where they did not do something better than we do it, think some thoughts better than we think, catch some inspiration from heights above our own. —Maria Mitchell

Whether you travel to another country or simply to another city or neighborhood, you're blessed to be able to get in your car, take a train, board a ship, or walk anywhere you want to go. You're free to travel, to live, and to breathe in new joys by the grace of God.

The LORD's majesty / will be there for us: / as a place of rivers, broad streams / where no boats will go, / no majestic ship will cross. —Isaiah 33:21

Lord, thank you that you go ahead of me and with me wherever I go...

WEEK 21 / DAY 5: *Free to Fail*

I haven't failed. I've found 10,000 ways that don't work.
— Benjamin Franklin

Do you give yourself the freedom to fail? Do you try things so big that unless God intervenes they are bound to fail? Failure and success are linked because one of them reminds you to keep trying and the other one gives you the way to get where you want to go. Keep trying and trusting. God knows the way for you.

I, the LORD, have called you for a good reason. / I will grasp your hand and guard you. —Isaiah 42:6

Lord, thank you for being with me, even when things have not worked out as I had planned...

WEEK 21 / DAY 6: *Express Yourself*

Of all the things you wear, your expression is the most important.
—Author unknown

Your facial expressions certainly tell people how you are feeling today. The beauty of it is that you are free to express the way you feel and share as much of those feelings as you choose. God always wants to know how you feel. He always wants to be your confidante.

The works of the LORD are magnificent; / they are treasured by all who desire them.
—Psalm 111:2

Lord, I love that I can express my heart and mind so freely to those who care about me and especially to you…

WEEK 21 / DAY 7: *To Think Out Loud*

All truly wise thoughts have been thought already thousands of times; but to make them truly ours, we must think them over again honestly, till they take root in our personal experience.
—Goethe

Imagine living in a world where you were not allowed to think your own thoughts, not free to express your ideas and feelings. God has blessed us with the freedom to think, to make choices, to come to him with anything that we wrestle with. He wants us to think out loud.

There isn't a word on my tongue, LORD, / that you don't already know completely.
—Psalm 139:4

Lord, I cherish you and thank you for the freedom to think freely and honestly…

Thankful for Extraordinary Teachers

Our critical day is not the very day of our death, but the whole course of life; I thank them that pray for me when my bell tolls; but I thank them much more, that catechize me, or preach to me, or instruct me how to live.
—*John Donne*

Those who serve as teachers in your life may not be associated with the place you went to high school or college. They may not have a degree in psychology or theology. They may simply be people who showed up at the right time with the kind of information that made a difference to you. They were drawn to you for a moment in time and walked with you long enough to help you take a new step.

Teachers may have a lot of life experience and have a good sense of the world because they've lived through it and survived it. Teachers may also be innocent children who say the exact thing that needs to be said and who make you smile because they are so profound.

God has blessed you with remarkable people to influence you, listen to you, and help you find your place and become strong. Be thankful for each one who taught you a valuable lesson and who gave you a nugget you can pass on to someone else. Those beautiful lessons learned help shape who you are and what you do. Thank God for all your wonderful teachers!

Teach us to number our days so we can have a wise heart. —Psalm 90:12

Lord, thank you for directing my steps with amazing teachers...

WEEK 22/ DAY 2: *Thankful for Mothers Who Guide by Example*

You have omitted to mention the greatest of my teachers—my mother. —Winston Churchill

Einstein said, "I never teach my pupils; I only attempt to provide the conditions in which they can learn."

Mothers are stunning teachers. They work hard to provide the best conditions for their children to learn about life and relationships. Those first life experiences that mothers provide can make all the difference in growing up and becoming the person you are today. It's always a good idea to be grateful for your mother and consider all she did to provide a loving environment for you, a place where you could safely learn to be yourself.

Like a newborn baby, desire the pure milk of the word. Nourished by it, you will grow into salvation. —1 Peter 2:2

Lord, thank you for all that I learned at my mother's knee…

WEEK 22/ DAY 3: *Becoming More*

Blessed is the influence of one true, loving soul on another.
—George Eliot

It's not always easy to want to stay in the training programs of life, to get that next degree or that final diploma. Yet nothing stands still. Growth means keeping up with a world that threatens to go on without you. The way we embrace life and opportunities makes all the difference in the person we become. Even the way others see us can be part of how we perceive ourselves. Goethe wrote, "Treat people as if they were what they ought to be and you help them become what they are capable of being."

Be thankful for those people who saw your potential and helped you see yourself more clearly. Without them, you might not be who you are today.

As you set yourselves apart by your obedience to the truth so that you might have genuine affection for your fellow believers, love each other deeply and earnestly.
—1 Peter 1:22

Lord, thank you for those people who saw more in me than I could see in myself…

WEEK 22/ DAY 4: *Learning from Nature*

The more I study nature, the more I am amazed at the Creator.
—Louis Pasteur

Once Adam and Eve left the garden, they had to learn to see the beauty around them in a new way. They had to try to see God's grace wherever they were. You have to do that as well. You have to learn from the world around you and seek the messages that make your path smoother and more enjoyable.

William Blake said, "The tree which moves some to tears of joy is, in the eyes of others, only a green thing which stands in the way." How will you choose to see the world today?

*Jesus answered, "I assure you, unless someone is born anew, it's not possible to see God's kingdom." —*John 3:3

Lord, help me see your kingdom with a grateful heart…

WEEK 22/ DAY 5: *Good Advice*

No gift is more precious than good advice. —Erasmus

Advice flows freely, wanted or not. Work through the gifts of advice that come your way and find the nuggets worth keeping and apply them to your life. When you do, they can serve you well.

As the Proverbs remind us, it's often useful to accept good advice. It helps strengthen our direction. Samuel Taylor Coleridge said, "Advice is like snow; the softer it falls, the longer it dwells upon, and the deeper it sinks into the mind." Be grateful for good advice that serves you well.

Teach the wise, and they will become wiser; / inform the righteous, and their learning will increase. —Proverbs 9:9

Father, I thank you for the wisdom that others have shared with me…

WEEK 22/ DAY 6: *Learning from Mistakes*

A life spent making mistakes is not only more honorable but more useful than a life spent doing nothing.
—George Bernard Shaw

It's not a question of whether you'll make mistakes, it's a question of what you'll do when you realize you've made one. Thomas Carlyle said, "Never let mistakes or wrong directions, of which every man falls into many, discourage you. There is precious instruction to be got by finding where you went wrong."

Looking back on your mistakes, maybe you can actually be grateful for them, knowing that those mistakes helped shape your thoughts and bring you to a new possibility. Be grateful for every mistake that teaches you a little more about yourself.

Commit your work to the LORD, and your plans will succeed. —Proverbs 16:3

Lord, thank you for turning me around when I've made mistakes and leading me forward again…

WEEK 22/ DAY 7: *Teachings from Doubt*

Too often we forget that the great men of faith reached the heights they did only by going through the depths. —Os Guinness

Sometimes it's not your determination that moves you toward a goal, it's your doubt. You may challenge yourself to keep trying in spite of your own sense of uncertainty. In that regard, doubt is a good teacher. It reminds you that it alone is not the final answer. Descartes once wrote, "If you would be a real seeker after truth, it is necessary that at least once in your life you doubt, as far as possible, all things." Since doubt may well serve as a catalyst inspiring you to move forward, it is a wise teacher.

You man of weak faith! Why did you begin to have doubts? —Matthew 14:31 (Jesus to Peter)

Lord, thank you for giving us the freedom to doubt, so that we can learn to trust more fully…

Thankful for Good Health

❧❧

More than anything you guard, / protect your mind, for life flows from it.
—Proverbs 4:23

God designed our bodies so that they were compatible with the environ-ment. He gave us every life-sustaining nutrient and chemical. He knew what we needed to grow healthy and strong. He provided for us so that we could live well on the earth and be able to carry out our personal life work.

Not only did God provide for our physical health, but he also works to pro-vide for our financial, spiritual, psychological, and emotional health as well. He knows us better than we know ourselves. He knows what we need before we even realize we are deprived.

As we seek to protect our physical health by exercising and eating well, let us also strive to strengthen our emotional and spiritual health. Thank God for all he does to sustain your well-being and give you an abundant life. Surrender your heart and mind to him.

A healthy body, a loving heart, and a grateful spirit are your richest gifts.
—Karen Moore

Lord, I am truly grateful that you have taken such good care of me, keeping me safe and free from illness…

WEEK 23/ DAY 2: *Fruits and Veggies*

For a long life ... breakfast like a king, lunch moderately, and dine like a pauper. —Author unknown

Whether you eat three meals a day or six small ones, or any other variation, the opportunity is there for you to eat healthy foods to protect your body. God loves you so much, he gave you a rich variety of options. You can select the low-hanging fruit and do well, or you can create gourmet delights. Give thanks for the bounty he has given you.

I am the living bread that came down from heaven. Whoever eats this bread will live forever, and the bread that I will give for the life of the world is my flesh. —John 6:51

Lord, thank you for giving yourself to be the bread of the world. Help me take care of the body you have given me to work in your service ...

WEEK 23/ DAY 3: *What Was I Thinking?*

Watch your thoughts; they become words. Watch your words; they become actions. Watch your actions; they become habits. Watch your habits; they become character. Watch your character; for it becomes your destiny! —Author unknown

Sometimes it's good to simply stop and take intentional notice of what it is you think about. What occupies your mind most days? What motivates you or drags you down? God wants you to have peace of mind. Thank him for being a God of peace and order and not of confusion. Think about it!

God isn't a God of disorder but of peace. —1 Corinthians 14:33

Lord, help me turn my thoughts toward you with loving gratitude for all you do for me ...

WEEK 23/ DAY 4: *An Ocean of Emotion*

God has not created man to be a stock or stone but has given him five senses and a heart of flesh, so that he loves his friends, is angry with his enemies, and commiserates with his dear friends in adversity. —Martin Luther

God created us for relationship. He wants us to feel each other's joys, each other's burdens, and his love. He wants us to share our hearts in the full spectrum of emotion. What a gift it is!

Be happy with those who are happy, and cry with those who are crying. —Romans 12:15

Lord, thank you that I can feel your love and grace...

WEEK 23/ DAY 5: *Making Healthy Choices*

Every moment you have a choice, regardless of what has happened before. Choose right now to move forward, positively and confidently into your incredible future. —Author unknown

You were given a brain, a heart, and a mind. With those came God's gift of choices, his willingness that you should seek him and seek your path in life. He gave you the opportunity through free will to become all that he designed you to be. What joy that brings!

Look here! Today I've set before you life and what's good versus death and what's wrong. —Deuteronomy 30:15

Lord, thank you for giving me the chance to make healthy choices...

WEEK 23/ DAY 6: *Of Mind and Spirit*

You no more need a day off from spiritual concentration in matters of your life than your heart needs a day off from beating. As you cannot take a day off morally and remain moral, you cannot take a day off spiritually and remain spiritual.
—Oswald Chambers

To be in optimum health, you need to be conscientious about the way you eat and about your willingness to exercise. Sometimes the idea of exercising fills you with dread, but when you do it, you feel better about yourself. Your spirit nudges you all the time to feed it and nurture it and give it a chance to help you understand the things of God more easily. Thank God for his persistent Spirit.

The one who searches hearts knows how the Spirit thinks, because he pleads for the saints, consistent with God's will. —Romans 8:27

Lord, thank you for giving us your kind and welcome Spirit...

WEEK 23/ DAY 7: *A Word to the Wise*

Words which do not give the light of Christ increase the darkness.
—Mother Teresa

When we're in a good place, emotionally and spiritually, we're much more able to bless others with our words. What we say either creates new possibility or destroys opportunity. Our words matter! Thank God when you use words that are kind and caring and wise.

To give an appropriate answer is a joy; how good is a word at the right time!
—Proverbs 15:23

Lord, I am always grateful when someone offers me encouraging words...

Thankful for Communication

The world will never starve for want of wonders, but for want of wonder.

—*G. K. Chesterton*

The fact that the world is shrinking is a wonder in itself, but what's caused us to recognize that more than anything is the proliferation of amazing technological breakthroughs. We can call our friends in faraway countries just as easily as we can call our neighbors. We can text with our kids, Skype our conference calls, and have real-time video conversations from our cell phones. Companies like Apple and Microsoft have catapulted us into the information age.

It wasn't that long ago when you could actually leave the house and not be able, without the use of a roadside telephone, to connect with your office or your family. Now, we're connected pretty much 24/7. We can jump onto the internet and discover remedies for illnesses, secrets of well-known chefs and their culinary delights, and nearly anything else we might hope to discover. The internet is the biggest library in the world and it's pretty much free and available to everyone.

We're finally in that place where God's Word can literally be heard by every person on the planet. That's communication at its finest.

God remembers his covenant forever. —Psalm 111:5

Lord, it is amazing to realize how easily we can talk to our neighbors and friends, and yet with no technology at all, we can talk to you anytime…

WEEK 24/ DAY 2: *Instant Messages*

Good news from a distant land is like cold water for a weary person. —Proverbs 25:25

Email has changed the way we communicate more than any other single invention. Sure a telephone is a good thing, but you can email anyone in the whole wide world in an instant. There's hardly a moment that passes that you don't have a chance to connect with someone near or far. What a blessing!

Be on the lookout for mercies. The more we look for them, the more of them we will see.... Better to lose count while naming your blessings than to lose your blessings to counting your troubles. —Author unknown

Lord, I do appreciate that I stay so well connected to others through my email address...

WEEK 24/ DAY 3: *The U.S. Mail*

You don't live in a world all alone. Your brothers are here, too. —Albert Schweitzer

If you grew up in decades before this one, you may remember how anxiously you waited for a special letter, or something you ordered through the U.S. Mail. You may remember going to the mailbox, hoping each time that the thing you most wanted would be there. Your mailbox was a reminder that you were not alone in the world.

Lord, you have been our help, generation after generation. —Psalm 90:1

Lord, thank you for the U.S. Mail. It still delivers joy...

WEEK 24/ DAY 4: *In Praise of the Internet*

A journey of a thousand sites begins with a single click.
—Author unknown

Maybe you can remember what your communication with others was like before the internet. If so, you may struggle now to imagine what life would be like without it. Instant connection, instant information, everything at your fingertips! That really is something to make your heart glad.

I want you to be wise about what's good, and innocent about what's evil.
—Romans 16:19

Lord, you have given us ways to fill our heads with worldly knowledge; help us also desire to fill our hearts with knowledge of you...

WEEK 24/ DAY 5: *Thankful for My Network*

No road is long with good company. —Turkish Proverb

We each rely pretty heavily on our own "network." It may be the people in our small group study, or those who volunteer for the same causes. It may be the ones you're linked to online or the ones you simply pass each day as you walk through the neighborhood. We're grateful for those who know us in even the smallest ways.

Make just and faithful decisions; show kindness and compassion to each other!
—Zechariah 7:9

Lord, I'm so grateful for all the people who surround me with love and friendship, my network of trust...

WEEK 24/ DAY 6: *Between Me and Thee*

*God never ceases to speak to us, but the noise of the world without
and the tumult of our passions within bewilder us and prevent us
from listening to him.* —François Fénelon

Sometimes the very best communication available to you is not the one that comes from checking your email, waiting for the postal service, or nodding at your neighbor as you drive down the street. Sometimes you get the most from a few quiet moments, one on one, with the Creator of the universe.

Samuel said, "Speak. Your servant is listening." —1 Samuel 3:10

Lord, I thank you and praise you that you listen so often to me; help me listen more to you...

WEEK 24/ DAY 7: *Coffee Chart*

*Good communication is just as stimulating as black coffee, and
just as hard to sleep after.* —Anne Morrow Lindbergh

We're grateful for those moments when we sit and contemplate the world with a great cup of coffee and a trusted friend. We could often sit for hours, measuring our joys and sorrows one sip at a time. Thank God that we become grounded in such a fine way.

Carry each other's burdens and so you will fulfill the law of Christ.
—Galatians 6:2

Lord, my favorite communication is always with a trusted friend, a cup of steaming coffee, and you...

Thankful for Dreams

Most people never run far enough on their first wind to find out they've got a second. Give your dreams all you've got and you'll be amazed at the energy that comes out of you.
—William James

Part of being human is the part of us that rises high above our circumstances, raising our hearts to the infinite possibility that can only be described as the place where our dreams reside. God knows the desires of your heart and wants you to be fulfilled, wants you to take advantage of the gifts he's given you to become more than you are today, to grow and change and dream.

You're God's dream come true in many ways, and your dreams matter because they are a reflection of what your Creator designed you to be, part of the mission you came to do, and part of the way others will come to glorify him. Be glad for your dreams and aspirations. Set your sights so high that they would surely fail if God did not intervene on your behalf. You're in this together, dreaming of life at its fullest. God loves the dreamer in you.

In the last days, God says, / I will pour out my Spirit on all people. / Your sons and daughters will prophesy. / Your young will see visions. / Your elders will dream dreams.
—Acts 2:17

Lord, thank you for keeping the dreams alive in me...

WEEK 25/ DAY 2: *Desires of Your Heart*

I'm the one who examines minds and hearts, and…I will give to each of you what your actions deserve. —Revelation 2:23

When God is with you, you can do anything. Your dreams come true and the desires of your heart can be fulfilled. Seek God with all your heart and he will bless you in ways that you cannot yet comprehend. Hold on to what is good and what is honorable, and he will come to you. Thanks be to God!

Desire is fulfilled through Determination, Effort, Sacrifice, Initiative, Responsibility, and Enthusiasm. —Author unknown

Lord, you know me so well and I thank you for giving me dreams, desires not yet extinguished that I can seek to fulfill with your help…

WEEK 25/ DAY 3: *Ushering In the Future*

Therefore, stop worrying about tomorrow, because tomorrow will worry about itself. Each day has enough trouble of its own. —Matthew 6:34

The future is always an open door for dreamers. It's the place where riddles of the universe, perplexing issues of the day, and stimulating ideas all come together. It's the place where our hearts dance optimistically even when our feet drag a bit waiting to be encouraged. Praise God that his blessings continue to flow and create new reasons to hope for a brighter tomorrow.

The future belongs to those who believe in the beauty of their dreams. —Eleanor Roosevelt

Lord, I am so grateful that my heart seeks all that you yet have for me in the future…

WEEK 25/ DAY 4: *Goal Tenders*

*Desire first and foremost God's kingdom and God's righteous-
ness, and all these things will be given to you as well.*
—Matthew 6:33

There's something about setting a new goal that inspires your spirit and motivates your every action. It stimulates you to think more positively and to seek more diligently to achieve the goal you've set. Truly, it is a gift of God to be inspired in a new direction, something blessedly deserving of thanks and praise.

A written down goal, in some way no one yet understands, tends to attract every ingredient it needs to realize it. —Author unknown

Lord, I am so truly grateful for the goals we've set together, dreams yet to be fulfilled…

⟨◈⟩

WEEK 25/ DAY 5: *With a Little Ambition*

*Aim to live quietly, mind your own business, and earn your own
living, just as I told you.* —1 Thessalonians 4:11

Your ambitions in life don't have to match those of anyone else. You may find you're not ambitious about climbing a corporate ladder, but you're set to move forward in your dreams to become a speaker or a teacher or a great mom. Ambition is a tender seed and if it is nurtured with love, it will indeed blossom.

The world stands aside to let anyone pass who knows where he is going.
—Author unknown

Lord, thank you for causing me to want more for my life, to desire all that you have for me…

WEEK 25/ DAY 6: *Aspire Higher*

If we hope for what we don't see, we wait for it with patience.
—Romans 8:25

Hope may not come with feathers, but it certainly gives wings to our desires and our dreams. Hope suggests that there's more than meets the eye in the world as we know it. We can truly aspire for something more, something higher, because that is what God wants for us.

Far away there in the sunshine are my highest aspirations. I may not reach them, but I can look up and see their beauty, believe in them, and try to follow where they lead.
—Louisa May Alcott

Lord, in loving gratitude I seek to know more of what you have for me, to follow my aspirations and dreams…

WEEK 25/ DAY 7: *It's Your Destiny!*

You are only a human being. Who do you think you are to talk back to God? Does the clay say to the potter, "Why did you make me like this?" Doesn't the potter have the power over the clay to make one pot for special purposes and another for garbage from the same lump of clay? —Romans 9:20-21

Your destiny is in God's hand because he is the one who formed you and gave you a purpose to fulfill. He had a dream for your life, a vision of what you would become, and he gave you all that you would need to accomplish the goal. Thank him that you are so fearfully and wonderfully made.

Be inspired with the belief that life is a great and noble calling; not a mean and groveling thing that we are to shuffle through as we can, but an elevated and lofty destiny.
—William E. Gladstone

Lord, I thank you for whatever I am destined to achieve, for the work that you alone began in me…

Thankful for God

But God shows his love for us, because while we were still sinners Christ died for us.
—Romans 5:8

Our intention this week is to focus on God and not so much on all the ways we recognize God in our lives. Here we'll thank him simply for being God, for loving us as we are, for protecting our hearts and minds and for giving us so much of himself. We'll thank him for his power in our lives, his love, his protection, and his saving grace. We'll thank God simply for being God!

We may not always understand or recognize God's influence in our lives, his gifts and his goodness. We may not understand his power or his holiness, but no matter, because he continues to reach out to us, his children.

God sees us as valuable and as wonderful. He sees our potential to grow and to change and to become. In that way, he truly acts as a parent, seeking our highest good and knowing we have all it takes to accomplish our dreams. Our hearts are overwhelmed by his initiative, his knowledge of our true selves, and his eagerness to know us better and to have us know him in return. Thank God and praise his name!

In his love he clothes us, enfolds us and embraces us; that tender love completely surrounds us, never to leave us. —Julian of Norwich

Lord, I am humbled by your complete and utter love for me…

WEEK 26/ DAY 2: *God's Glory*

Declare God's glory among the nations; / declare his wondrous works among all people / because the LORD *is great and so worthy of praise.* —1 Chronicles 16:24-25

God's glory is a fact. Sometimes we offer humble thanks and praise. Sometimes we do nothing. God loves us so much that he accepts our attempts to give him glory even when we don't truly understand what it means. He looks forward to any approach we might make to be with him in any way possible.

A man can no more diminish God's glory by refusing to worship him than a lunatic can put out the sun by scribbling the word darkness *on the walls of his cell.* —C. S. Lewis

Lord, let me ever seek ways to give you thanks and glory...

WEEK 26/ DAY 3: *God's Goodness*

Who among you will give your children a stone when they ask for bread? —Matthew 7:9

We often remind ourselves that God is good. When we do, if we really think about it, we realize the truth of that statement. We know that when we come to him and bare our souls and ask for the things we need, he hears us and immediately acts for our good. We are indeed thankful for his goodness to us.

Our heavenly Father never takes anything from his children unless he means to give them something better. —George Muller

Lord, you're incredible! Your goodness to me is without measure...

WEEK 26/ DAY 4: *God's Love*

Whoever is wise will pay attention to these things, / carefully considering the LORD's faithful love. —Psalm 107:43

God loves you so much. He sees all that you go through and stands by your side. He hears you when you call and he answers according to his will and purpose and according to your good. No one could love you more! Nothing can separate you from his enduring love.

God loves us not because of who we are, but because of who he is!
—Author unknown

Lord, I am sure that I can scarcely take in the ways that you love me...

WEEK 26/ DAY 5: *God's Mercy*

He shows mercy to everyone, from one generation to the next, who honors him as God. —Luke 1:50

Honor God with all your heart. Let him know how much you appreciate his tender mercy and grace. He offers you a chance to be new each morning, letting yesterday melt away and today bringing opportunities for great joy. He sees your heart and has compassion on your soul.

Among the attributes of God, although they are all equal, mercy shines with even more brilliance than justice. —Miguel de Cervantes

Lord, I realize you've extended great mercy to me...

WEEK 26/ DAY 6: *God's Nature*

I am the alpha and the omega, the first and the last, the beginning and the end. —Revelation 22:13

God is! As the Creator, he began all that is, all that we know and all that we have yet to know. He is everlasting, from age to age, never changing, steadfast and true. His Word remains forever. Our hearts fill with gratitude because he chooses to love and guide us each day.

The Father of all … is all understanding, all spirit, all thought, all hearing, all seeing, all light, and the whole source of everything good. —Irenaeus

Lord, it is with awe and wonder that I come to you…

WEEK 26/ DAY 7: *God's Presence*

The LORD said, "Go out and stand at the mountain before the LORD. The LORD is passing by." A very strong wind tore through the mountains and broke apart the stones before the LORD. But the LORD wasn't in the wind. After the wind, there was an earthquake. But the LORD wasn't in the earthquake. / After the earthquake, there was a fire. But the LORD wasn't in the fire. After the fire, there was a sound. Thin. Quiet. —1 Kings 19:11-12

Eijah went to stand in the presence of the Lord. He observed, from the protection of a cave, that the Lord was passing by and the ground shook and the mountain trembled. Finally, Elijah heard it, the still, small voice of God. At last, he stood in the Lord's presence. How grateful we are when we feel his presence in our lives.

We should always honor and reverence Him as if we were always in His bodily presence. —Thomas à Kempis

Lord, I am grateful that you are willing to allow me to come into your presence and that I can find you…

Thankful God Is in Control

I am the LORD, the God of all living things! Is anything too hard for me?
—Jeremiah 32:27

Most of us are groomed from infancy to learn to stand on our own two feet, to become independent and to make our own paths. Certainly aspects of that kind of nurturing are useful to us as we grow and mature. In matters of faith, however, the objective is somewhat different. In faith, we come to rely on the One who is in authority. Only God knows our purpose and the work he designed us to do. He looks for us to surrender to him, to be willing to put our lives in his hands and to allow him to work with us from the inside out.

As one writer put it, "Either God is totally sovereign, ordaining, ruling, and disposing of all things as he will, or he has no control over anything and faith in him is an utter absurdity." As we seek his will in our lives, let us be willing to give him complete control so that we may live in harmony with him and with one another.

To say that God is sovereign is to say that His power is superior to every other form of expression of power; it is to say that God is completely free of external influences so that He does what He chooses, as He chooses, when He chooses. —James Bordwine

Lord, thank you for being in control of my life…

WEEK 27 / DAY 2: *The World View*

Don't be conformed to the patterns of this world, but be trans-
formed by the renewing of your minds so that you can figure out
what God's will is—what is good and pleasing and mature.
—Romans 12:2

As grateful as we are to be in the world, to have a community of love, an opportunity to grow and thrive, and a place to call our own, we can have even greater confidence in knowing our Creator is in complete control. He started all that we see for his own purposes and he will fulfill his own mission.

Our work here is brief but its reward is eternal. Do not be disturbed by the clamor of the world, which passes away like a shadow. —Clare of Assisi

Lord, thank you that my life rests in your hands…

WEEK 27 / DAY 3: *Whistle While You Work*

Think about the things above and not things on earth.
—Colossians 3:2

Work can be consuming. It eats up your days and causes them to melt into each other. Before long, they become years or decades and you find yourself wondering what happened to your life. When did you lose sight of all that you could be or might have been? Give God control over your life today.

Two things rob people of their peace of mind: work unfinished and work not yet begun. —Author unknown

Lord, thank you for the work that you've called me to do…

WEEK 27/ DAY 4: *All God's Children*

Whoever welcomes one such child in my name welcomes me.
—Matthew 18:5

Whether we're parents with biological children or not, we're parents of any child in need, any child God places in our care in some way, because as adults we are responsible for the children of this world regardless of heritage or creed. God expects us to care for his children with hearts full of gratitude for them and for him.

The one who helps children helps humanity with an immediateness which no other help given to human creatures in any other stage of human life can possibly give again.
—Phillips Brooks

Lord, the children of this world need you so desperately, and I am grateful you watch over them…

WEEK 27/ DAY 5: *Designed for Relationship*

This is my commandment: love each other just as I have loved you. —John 15:12

God designed us to be in relationship to him and to one another. He works within us to do good deeds for others and to value everyone. He causes each of us to minister to the other. He called us to be in community.

Use your head to handle yourself, your heart to handle others.
—Author unknown

Lord, thank you for the gift of caring, the opportunity to minister to those around me…

WEEK 27 / DAY 6: *Fear Not!*

There is no fear in love, but perfect love drives out fear.
—1 John 4:18

The Bible often uses phrases like "Do not fear!" or "Take courage!" because God is in control. God's love for us and our love for him drives fear away. We know that he works for our good in all things and in all circumstances. What joy that understanding brings to the heart!

Fear knocked at the door. Faith answered and no one was there.
—Author unknown

Lord, thank you that I can leave all fears at your feet, knowing you are always in control…

WEEK 27 / DAY 7: *Lighting Candles*

Walk while you have the light so that darkness doesn't overtake you. —John 12:35

Thank God that he controls the darkness, the places in our lives where we are not yet fully ready to be exposed. He knows what we hope to accomplish and all that we desire, and he takes every opportunity to guide us in the right direction. He is our light.

If you're not lighting any candles, don't complain about the dark.
—Author unknown

Lord, thank you for lighting my way and allowing me to be a spark of light to others…

Thankful for Choices

Pay attention! I am setting blessing and curse before you right now: the blessing if you obey the LORD your God's commandments that I am giving you right now, but the curse if you don't obey.

—Deuteronomy 11:26-28

We love having choices! We love to go to a restaurant and be offered a menu that tantalizes every taste bud and enhances our opportunity to be served gourmet delights. We like going to bookstores and seeing row after row and shelf after shelf teeming with information that can lure us in and satiate our curiosity on any subject under the sun.

God filled the world with choices because with each one, we become more fully aware of who we are and what we might become. With those choices we become more responsible beings. Eleanor Roosevelt said, "One's philosophy is not best expressed in words; it is expressed in the choices one makes. In the long run, we shape our lives and we shape ourselves. The process never ends until we die. And the choices we make are ultimately our responsibility."

Nearly every moment a new choice presents itself. Go to church today or stay home. Clean the closet or watch TV. Write a note to a friend or read a book. It's endless. Our job is to give God the best opportunity to use us in the choices we make no matter what they are.

Lord, though it's not always easy to make choices, I thank you for them…

WEEK 28/ DAY 2: *Choosing to Live*

*My days are swifter than a weaver's shuttle; / they reach their
end without hope. / Remember that my life is wind.*
—Job 7:6-7

We recognize with Job how fleeting life is, how quickly it melts away taking
our dreams and our fine intentions with it. Perhaps one of God's gifts is that our
span of life should be short enough to give us a taste of all that he has, but not
so long that we forget him in the process. Choose to bring God into every area
of your life today.

*Take the life you've been given / And give it your best, / Think positive thoughts /
And let God do the rest.* —Author unknown

Lord, thank you for giving me this day…

WEEK 28/ DAY 3: *Choosing to Work*

Then people go off to their work, to do their work until evening.
—Psalm 104:23

God has blessed you with the opportunity to choose your vocation, your
profession. You can work as much or as little as you want because you have the
freedom to make those choices. God respects your work and blesses all that
you do because it's part of fulfilling your mission and your dreams.

*All labor that uplifts humanity has dignity and importance and should be under-
taken with painstaking excellence.* —Martin Luther King, Jr.

Lord, I thank you for the work I do…

WEEK 28/ DAY 4: *Choosing an Education*

Take my instruction rather than silver, knowledge rather than choice gold. —Proverbs 8:10

We think of formal education as a thing to be desired, and it is, but all of life brings the choice to learn from it. We can choose to benefit by the education we receive from all the teachers in our midst and from God. When we do, we gain real wisdom.

Some books are to be tasted, others to be swallowed, and some few to be chewed and digested. —Francis Bacon

Lord, thank you that I keep learning…

WEEK 28/ DAY 5: *Choosing Entertainment*

I say to myself, / I wish I had wings like a dove! / I'd fly away and rest. —Psalm 55:6

You work hard and you deserve to rest. Whether you rest by taking a nap or playing a round of golf or simply curling up with a good book, your body needs the down time. Happily, you are free to choose the moment and the way that you will spend a little leisure time. Thank God for those moments.

All joy (as distinct from mere pleasure, still more amusement) emphasizes our pilgrim status; always reminds, beckons, awakens desire. —C. S. Lewis

Lord, I thank you for the moments to simply do things I enjoy…

WEEK 28/ DAY 6: *Choosing a Partner*

But a helper perfect for him was nowhere to be found.
—Genesis 2:20

Adam and Eve were literally made for each other. They didn't have to go through the effort of looking for a mate because they were perfectly matched. The rest of us have to approach the process a bit differently, searching for someone who will fit perfectly into our lives. God graciously gives us the choice.

There is no more lovely, friendly or charming relationship, communion or company, than a good marriage. —Martin Luther

Lord, thank you for giving me the choice of discovering a loving partner...

WEEK 28/ DAY 7: *Choosing Jesus*

Christ Jesus came into the world to save sinners.
—1 Timothy 1:15

God doesn't force us to love his Son. He gives us a chance to choose. God chose us and we get to choose him right back. It's a matter of love. May your heart overflow with gratitude to the One who keeps coming back and giving you a chance to choose him yet again.

Salvation is God's way of making us real people. —Augustine of Hippo

Lord, thank you for your Son Jesus...

Thankful for Healing

A joyful heart helps healing, but a broken spirit dries up the bones.
—Proverbs 17:22

Imagine a body that did not heal itself. Happily our Creator knew that we would bruise our knees, fall from the swings, and trip over things when we were growing up. He knew we would have the measles, get a toothache, or cough all night. He knew those things would come and so he gave us miraculous bodies that have the ability to heal. We can be broken and be restored.

Fortunately, healing isn't simply a matter of bones and bruises. It's also a matter of life and relationships, of bruised egos and broken hearts. It's a matter of forgiving and trying and being disappointed. It's a matter of maintaining a healthy life style that makes it possible to have a healthy body and strong mind. God is interested in every aspect of your being and he wants every part of you to be healthy, so he designed you so that you could heal from whatever life might bring your way. He does not want you to suffer from a broken spirit that may cause both your bones and your mind to become brittle. Thank God that you have such a marvelous body, designed to survive, designed to protect, and designed to heal you at every stage of life.

He who enjoys good health is rich, though he knows it not. —Italian proverb

Thank you, Lord, for giving me a body, mind, and spirit that can be healed…

WEEK 29/ DAY 2: *A Mind That Matters*

More than anything you guard, protect your mind, for life flows from it. —Proverbs 4:23

You have a sound mind. You are bright and energetic and kind. You are a loving example of what God does when he heals a life and brings a child into his fold. You are strong and you make him proud. Thank God for giving you a beautiful heart and mind.

Choose to have a vigorous mind rather than a vigorous body. —Pythagoras

Lord, I am grateful you have given me a strong mind…

WEEK 29/ DAY 3: *Healing the Heart*

All things are from him and through him and for him. May the glory be to him forever. Amen. —Romans 11:36

Everything comes from God, and the quickest route to renewing our hearts and minds comes from thanking him for all circumstances. When your heart is hurting, take it to him for healing. He alone can release you from the sadness you might feel. He alone can help you stand again.

It is only with the heart that one can see rightly; what is essential is invisible to the eye. —Antoine de Saint-Exupery

Lord, thank you for healing my heart…

WEEK 29/ DAY 4: *Healing Finances*

Tell people who are rich at this time not to become egotistical and not to place their hope on their finances, which are uncertain. Instead, they need to hope in God, who richly provides everything for our enjoyment. —1 Timothy 6:17

God knows what you need. Your bank account may rise and fall, your stocks may soar or fold, but God continues to walk with you with the same desire, that you should experience life abundantly, that you should have all that you need. Praise him and thank him for his constant love.

Making money is necessary for daily living, but money-making is apt to degenerate into money-loving and then the deceitfulness of riches enters into and spoils the spiritual life. —W. H. Griffith Thomas

Lord, you know what I need. I thank you for providing for me and healing my finances…

WEEK 29/ DAY 5: *Healing Relationships*

I was hungry and you gave me food to eat. I was thirsty and you gave me a drink. I was a stranger and you welcomed me. —Matthew 25:35

God puts you in the midst of others so that you can grow and become strong. Sometimes you'll be in relationships that cause you to feel bruised or even broken. Sometimes you'll be in relationships with healers and givers, those who are kind beyond measure. Thank God for the people who help you heal the difficult relationships.

A feeling of good will toward others is the strongest magnet for drawing good will from others. —Lord Chesterfield

Lord, thank you for those people who bring joy and healing to my relationships…

WEEK 29/ DAY 6: *Healing the Earth*

You will not make the land in which you live unclean, the land in the middle of which I reside. —Numbers 35:34

God made everything we see and he saw that it was good. Just as he made our bodies to heal, he made the earth to heal as well as long as we take care of it. We are its protectors and its benefactors. Thank God that he continues to heal the planet.

God creates out of nothing. Therefore, until a man is nothing God can make nothing out of him. —Martin Luther

Lord, thank you for making something out of me and for giving us a planet that continues to heal and sustain life...

WEEK 29/ DAY 7: *Healing from Natural Disasters*

The mountains quake because of him; / the hills melt away. / The earth heaves before him— / the world and all who dwell in it. —Nahum 1:5

Sometimes we call natural disasters that befall the planet "acts of God." Whether they are acts of God or natural responses to shifts and changes of the planet itself, we know that ultimately God seeks to help us heal from those tremendous life-altering events. Thank God that he is with us in all that we experience on this planet.

At the timberline where the storms strike with the most fury, the sturdiest trees are found. —Hudson Taylor

Lord, thank you for stepping in when disaster strikes anywhere on this planet...

Thankful for the Holidays

❧

This is the day the LORD acted; / we will rejoice and celebrate in it!
—Psalm 118:24

No matter what the holiday is, it's designed to be a form of celebration, honoring a certain event in our history, reminding us of the mystery and the joy of life, bringing us through the year with a sense of order and completeness. The Christian calendar alone offers us a beautiful way to keep remembering our Lord and all he did for us. From the celebration of his birthday in December and hearing the angel's stories of glory when his star appeared over Bethlehem, to the anticipation of a New Year, we delight in holidays.

The New Year fills us with hope again, triggering our desires to pray more, read the Word more, and be more of what God imagined us to be. We send each other valentines because love is the desire of every human heart, and then we fall on our knees at Easter with gratitude that Jesus died for us and rose again. By Thanksgiving, we know that it has been a good year and that we have any number of reasons to be grateful.

The life without festival is a long road without an inn. —Democritus of Abdera

Lord, thank you for the days in the year that cause us to stop and reflect more fully on all that we have…

WEEK 30/ DAY 2: *The Flag and the Fourth of July*

When immigrants live in your land with you, you must not cheat them. Any immigrant who lives with you must be treated as if they were one of your citizens. You must love them as yourself.
—Leviticus 19:33-34

America has long been a country that welcomes people from around the globe into her borders, offering freedom and rest. We live in the land of opportunity, and even today we have more freedom to be ourselves and to live as we choose than any nation on this planet. One of God's great gifts to us is about honoring each other.

All human beings are born free and equal in dignity and rights.
—Declaration of Human Rights, 1948

Lord, I know I am blessed beyond measure to live in America...

WEEK 30/ DAY 3: *The Gift of Christmas*

Your savior is born today in David's city. He is Christ the Lord.
—Luke 2:11

No matter what time of year it is now, thoughts of Christmas evoke images of starry, snowy nights, carolers, and homemade cookies. Each of us has a different idea of what it means to celebrate Christmas, but God had just one idea, to give us his Son, to lead us safely back home again. Thanks be to God!

Christ came when all things were growing old. He made them new.
—Augustine of Hippo

Lord, I will forever be grateful that you were born for me...

WEEK 30/ DAY 4: *New Year, New You Again!*

My whole being waits for my Lord— / more than the night watch waits for morning; / yes, more than the night watch waits for morning! —Psalm 130:6

There's always something wonderful about the beginning of a new year. It comes with a renewed sense of hope and intention. It gives us a feeling of being back in control of our aspirations. It causes us to wait with more patience for the Lord. This hope alone is enough to renew our gratitude.

The beginning is the most important part of the work. —Plato

Lord, I am truly delighted to look at the hope a new year brings and to celebrate…

WEEK 30/ DAY 5: *It's About Love*

Pursue love, and use your ambition to try to get spiritual gifts.
—1 Corinthians 14:1

We celebrate a number of holidays designed to remind us of love. Valentine's Day certainly has that focus, along with Sweetest Day. We might also add Mother's Day and Father's Day to this mix and even Christmas. Our greatest need is to love and be loved. As a response to that love, we go on to pursue even greater spiritual gifts. Thank God that he loves us so!

We are all born for love. It is the principle of existence, and its only end.
—Benjamin Disraeli

Lord, thank you for your love and the gift of love from others…

WEEK 30/ DAY 6: *He Rose Again!*

After Jesus said these things, as they were watching, he was lifted up and a cloud took him out of their sight. —Acts 1:9

How grateful we are for God's gift of salvation. We did not earn it. We may not even have known we needed it, but God did and so he provided a lamb, a sacrifice for our good. Thank you, Jesus!

She sat and wept, and with her untressed hair / She wiped the feet she was blest to touch;/ And He wiped off the soiling despair / From her sweet soul because she loved so much. —Dante Gabriel Rosetti

Lord, I know I don't understand your great love for me, but I thank you for it…

WEEK 30/ DAY 7: *Of Feasts and Thanksgiving!*

Give thanks in every situation because this is God's will for you in Christ Jesus. Don't suppress the Spirit.
—1 Thessalonians 5:18-19

Many of our ancestors gathered together when they reached their new home in America, uncertain as they were of what might be ahead. They gathered for one purpose, to thank God for leading them safely. A feast of gratitude makes the spirit soar!

Every blessing that God confers upon us perishes through our carelessness, if we are not prompt and active in giving thanks. —John Calvin

Lord, I pour out my gratitude to you today for…

Thankful for the Word of God

All human life on the earth is like grass, / and all human glory is
like a flower in a field. / The grass dries up and its flower falls off,
/ but the Lord's word endures forever.
—1 Peter 1:24

T his poem, "My Bible and I," from an unknown author, explains our gratitude for the Bible, our desire to cling to it and know more about it.

My Bible and I
We've traveled together through life's rugged way,
Over land and water, by night and by day:
To travel without it, I never would try;
 We keep close together, my Bible and I.
In sorrow, it's proved my comfort and joy,
In weakness a tower that none can destroy,
God's Word then directs me to Him in the sky,
And nothing can part us, my Bible and I.
If evil temptations come into view,
And I in my weakness don't know what to do,
On Christ, my true strength, I've been taught to rely
And so we stay close, my Bible and I.
And when in His glory, my Lord I behold,
With all the redeemed gathered safe in the fold,
My Bible and I close companions will be
For God's Word lives forever, all eternity.
—Adapted from unknown author

The Bible contains light to direct you, food to support you, and comfort to cheer you.
It is the traveler's guide, the pilgrim's staff, the pilot's compass, the soldier's sword, and
the Christian's character. —Author unknown

Lord, I am forever indebted to your Word and to you…

WEEK 31 / DAY 2: *The Trusted Resource*

Most important, you must know that no prophecy of scripture represents the prophet's own understanding of things, because no prophecy ever came by human will. Instead, men and women led by the Holy Spirit spoke from God. —2 Peter 1:20-21

What if we thought the Bible was only a good book, a journal of history or a poetic form of praise? What if we did not realize that it is indeed the Word of God, captured by writers so that generations could come to know more of their Creator? Happily, we are blessed to know we can trust God's Word!

Authority resides in God's inspired Word (the Bible) interpreted by God's Spirit operating through Spirit-taught human agents. —M. F. Unger

Lord, thank you that I can trust completely in your Word…

WEEK 31 / DAY 3: *Sacred Influence*

Your word is a lamp before my feet and a light for my journey. / I have sworn, and I fully mean it: / I will keep your righteous rules. —Psalm 119:105-6

As you read passages in the Word today, let them have their way with you, influencing your thoughts and actions. Let them slip into all you do and make each moment a sacred one. You'll have a glorious day!

God did not write a book and send it by messenger to be read at a distance by unaided minds. He spoke a Book and lives in His spoken words, constantly speaking his words and causing the power of them to persist across the years. —A. W. Tozer

Lord, I thank you that your Word guides me today…

WEEK 31/ DAY 4: *For Further Inspiration!*

Every scripture is inspired by God and is useful for teaching, for showing mistakes, for correcting, and for training character, so that the person who belongs to God can be equipped to do everything that is good. —2 Timothy 3:16-17

Need a little inspiration today? Sometimes you don't even know what you need, but your heavenly Father does, and he provides clues, tips, and direct revelation to help you make your way in the world. God knows, even before you do, what will help you and lovingly provides the necessary inspiration.

I know the Bible is inspired because it finds me at a greater depth of my being than any other book. —Samuel Taylor Coleridge

Lord, I'm grateful that you inspire my heart and mind every day...

WEEK 31/ DAY 5: *What Does That Verse Mean?*

Help me understand what your precepts are about / so I can contemplate your wondrous works! —Psalm 119:27

The Bible is a personal guide in that the Holy Spirit guides you through it, helping you interpret what you read so that it applies to your life. It's a living document and you can find yourself within its pages each time you pick it up. Thank God you can trust his Holy Spirit to guide you even when theology confuses you.

In 1728, potatoes were outlawed in Scotland because they were not mentioned in the Bible. —Author unknown

Lord, thank you that I have to work sometimes to understand your word...

WEEK 31 / DAY 6: *God's Purpose/My Purpose*

Train yourself for a holy life! While physical training has some
value, training in holy living is useful for everything.
—1 Timothy 4:7-8

God's purpose in giving you his living Word, his manuscript for the way to an abundant life, was that he knew you'd be lost without it. He directs your path and your plans. He seeks to help you fulfill your life purpose.

The Bible was given to bear witness to one God, Creator and Sustainer of the universe, through Christ, Redeemer of sinful man. It presents one continuous story—that of human redemption. —M. F. Unger

Lord, thank you for helping me to live intentionally for you ...

WEEK 31 / DAY 7: *The Wisdom Factor*

The beginning of wisdom: Get wisdom! Get understanding
before anything else. —Proverbs 4:7

You are wise to seek to know more of God, to wander through the pages of his Word hoping to grasp gentle nuggets to guide your way. The more you seek of him, the easier it will be to discover him in every area of your life. He is always there, hoping you are wise enough to desire more of him each day.

Nobody ever outgrows Scripture; the book widens and deepens with our years.
—C. H. Spurgeon

Lord, thank you for granting me enough wisdom to desire more of your Word ...

Thankful for Success

❧

As long as he sought the LORD, God gave him success.
—*2 Chronicles 26:5*

Y ou probably have an image of success or at least of what would make you
feel that you had succeeded at something. That image may even be different from the one you hold when you imagine the success of others. You
might assume that the winner of a lottery has a measure of success. You might
believe an actor with a starring role has achieved something monumental. You
might believe that others have success and you don't.

The fact is that you are very successful at life. You have navigated its waters
with a degree of skill and confidence. You can participate in your job, in your
home life, or at school in substantial ways. You have friends to share your joys
and people who love you. All of these things can be counted as the successes in
your life.

As you look at what makes you feel successful this week, remember to thank
God for putting you right where you are at this very moment. He has great
plans for you.

*The heights by great men reached and kept / Were not attained by sudden flight, /
But they, while their companions slept, / Were toiling upward in the night.*
—Henry Wadsworth Longfellow

Lord, thank you for all the ways you allow me to measure success…

WEEK 32/ DAY 2: *Little Victories*

Shout triumphantly to the LORD, all the earth! / Serve the LORD
with celebration! /Come before him with shouts of joy!
—Psalm 100:1-2

Praise God today for all the little victories in your life. Perhaps you've triumphed over an addiction, managed to keep all your bills paid on time, or committed to and then completed your exercise program. Reward yourself for those victories and they will lead you on to greater success.

Life is made up of small pleasures. Happiness is made up of those tiny successes—
the big ones come too infrequently. If you don't have all those zillions of tiny successes,
the big ones don't mean anything. —Norman Lear

Lord, I know that on any given day I have succeeded in some small way and I'm grateful…

WEEK 32/ DAY 3: *Momentary Greatness*

Let my whole being bless the LORD / and never forget all his good
deeds; / how God forgives all your sins,/ heals all your sickness,
/saves your life from the pit, /crowns you with faithful love and
compassion, / and satisfies you with plenty of good things.
—Psalm 103:2-5

You've been blessed with significant achievements. You've become educated, you've connected to the social fabric of the world, and you've managed to win the day. God is thrilled with your efforts and your hard work. His good deeds have brought your desires to fruition. Bless his name!

Life affords no greater pleasure than overcoming obstacles. —Author unknown

Lord, I know that I have not achieved anything without your will that it be so…

WEEK 32 / DAY 4: *True Wealth*

Then Jesus said to his disciples, "I assure you that it will be very
hard for a rich person to enter the kingdom of heaven."
—Matthew 19:23

You may think the successful people in the world are the ones with big
houses and even bigger bank accounts. Perhaps those things are a measure of
success, and yet the wealth of a people on earth does not necessarily equip
them for an easy ride into heaven. Thank God for your financial position and
that he is near you in all you do.

If you want to feel rich, just count all the things you have that money can't buy. —
Author unknown

Lord, I confess that I look at those who have accumulated wealth and imagine they are more successful than I am. Help me be grateful for what I have and
look only to you for my measure of success…

WEEK 32 / DAY 5: *Succeeding at Life*

Turn your ear and hear the words of the wise; / focus your mind
on my knowledge./ It will be pleasant if you keep the words in
you, / if you have them ready on your lips.
—Proverbs 22:17-18

Succeeding at life has more to do with your attitude and wisdom than it
does with your circumstances. You may not have worldly goods, but you may
have an abundance of character and faithfulness. Life offers challenges and no
matter what they might be, God offers to be there in the midst of them.

I asked God for all things, that I might enjoy life. God gave life, that I might enjoy
all things. —Author unknown

Lord, I thank you for sticking with me through all life's challenges and helping me overcome and succeed…

WEEK 32/ DAY 6: *Success Comes in Cans*

Commit your work to the LORD, and your plans will succeed.
—Proverbs 16:3

Whether or not you succeed often depends on two things, your willingness to put the work you plan to do into God's hands, and your willingness to really believe you can accomplish your goal. God can always help you receive when your heart is full of him and you truly believe.

Success comes in cans, failure comes in can'ts. —Author unknown

Lord, thank you for giving me a "can-do" attitude…

WEEK 32/ DAY 7: *Doing or Being*

Whatever you are capable of doing, do with all your might because there's no work, thought, knowledge, or wisdom in the grave. —Ecclesiastes 9:10

The Ecclesiastes writer hit the nail on the head when he reminded us to keep going, keep doing all that we can while we have the opportunity. The time of that opportunity will end. It's been said that we are human beings, not "human doings," but we succeed the most when we manage to "be" in the presence of our Creator and "do" what he would have us do.

I firmly believe that your finest hour is that moment when you have worked your heart out for a good cause and then lie exhausted on the field of battle, victorious. —Vince Lombardi (adapted)

Lord, thank you for helping me succeed by the things I do…

Thankful for Failure

❧

Take your ways to heart. You have sown much, but it has brought little.
—Haggai 1:5-6

Perhaps it doesn't exactly resonate with you to be thankful for those times when your plans fell through or you didn't succeed as you had hoped. Maybe you were passed over for a well-deserved promotion, or were laid off through no real fault of your own. Maybe your marriage fell apart or your kids rebelled. It isn't hard to find fault with yourself or to keep account of the times when things didn't go your way. The hard part is learning from those experiences, taking the good parts of them, and moving on.

The fact is you are always a success in God's eyes. You're always on top of your game because he sees you as a perfect design, totally becoming all that he dreamed for you. When we fall short of the mark we set for ourselves, we disappoint ourselves more than we disappoint our Creator. Sure, he may wonder at our choices and hope that a lesson will be learned, but in the end, he forgives and he moves on. He wants you to do the same.

Whatever strikes you as a failure in your life is simply an event like any other. You have hundreds of successes, and making the effort, no matter what the outcome, is often the greatest success of all. Be thankful for all you learn when something feels like a failure to you.

Failure is the opportunity to begin again more intelligently. —Henry Ford

Lord, I thank you that you are with me even when I have failed in some measure…

WEEK 33/ DAY 2: *Short of the Goal*

Think about the things above and not things on earth.
—Colossians 3:2

Whenever you miss the mark or fall short of the goal you have set, see if you can look at your seeming success or failure in this way. Did you fall short of God's will for you, his purpose for your life? Or did this setback actually bring you closer to him, seeking his help to help you be stronger as you approach the goal again? He's there for you.

To see God is the promised goal of all our actions and the promised height of all our joys. —Augustine of Hippo

Lord, thank you for being with me and helping me…

WEEK 33/ DAY 3: *"I'm So Mad at Myself"*

No one can receive anything unless it is given from heaven.
—John 3:27

When you make a mess of something, your first response may well be to simply feel angry. You might feel angry at yourself more than you are at anyone else when things don't go well. The fact is that some of your goals may not be aligned with what God wants for you right now. Even when the goal is a good one, it must be achieved at the right time. Be thankful God knows when the time is right for you to succeed.

First build a proper goal. That proper goal will make it easy, almost automatic, to build a proper you. —Goethe

Lord, I do get upset with myself when things don't happen as I plan them. Thank you for knowing what is best for me…

WEEK 33/ DAY 4: *"How Could I Have Done That?"*

I have no greater joy than this: to hear that my children are living according to the truth. —3 John 4

Sometimes you make choices that you know are really not going to bring good results. You might shop more than your budget really allows or work more than you should and not get enough sleep, or you might eat dessert too often. Whatever it is, you can't believe you made that choice. Don't beat yourself up! Thank God you can choose again.

Choose, decide, look at the results and choose again. Wisdom comes in making a better choice the next time. —Karen Moore

Lord, thank you for giving me opportunities to make better choices…

WEEK 33/ DAY 5: *Failing to Say the Right Thing*

We all make mistakes often, but those who don't make mistakes with their words have reached full maturity. —James 3:2

Speaking up appropriately and confidently is not always easy. Putting in a right word, offering verbal support to a friend or family member, helping someone see more clearly by giving good advice, these are the things we can choose to do. Sometimes we reflect on moments when we had a chance, perhaps to truly make a difference and we didn't do it. Thank God for every chance he gives you to lift up the heart of someone else.

Words which do not give the light of Christ increase the darkness.
—Mother Teresa

Lord, thank you for guiding me to say the right thing…

WEEK 33/ DAY 6: *Yipes! Another Mistake!*

The LORD looks down from heaven on humans / to see if anyone is wise, / to see if anyone seeks God, / but all of them have turned bad./ Everyone is corrupt. / No one does good—not even one person! —Psalm 14:2-3

We know that we need Jesus for God to see the things that are good about us. We are grateful that he accepts our humble efforts and searches our hearts. When he does, he can truly see how hard we try, even when we make mistakes. Happily, he makes us new every morning and gives us another chance to do better.

A life spent making mistakes is not only more honorable, but more useful than a life spent doing nothing. —George Bernard Shaw

Lord, I am so thankful that you forgive my mistakes…

WEEK 33/ DAY 7: *Breaking Down, Breaking Up!*

As far as east is from west— / that's how far God has removed our sin from us./ Like a parent feels compassion for their children—that's how the LORD feels compassion for those who honor him. —Psalm 103:12-13

God knows we do wrong things. He knows we sometimes fail at work or at relationships with our spouses, our children, or even our friends. Sometimes we break away from those we love. May your heart fill with gratitude each time you realize you are not alone even in your failures.

Forgiveness does not mean the cancellation of all consequences of wrongdoing. It means the refusal on God's part to let our guilty past affect his relationship with us. —Author unknown

Lord, knowing you're always there for me, even when I've failed in ways that disappoint us both, makes me grateful…

Thankful for Imagination

~∞~

In the dream, a vision of the night, / when deep sleep falls upon humans, during their slumber on a bed, / then he opens people's ears.
—Job 33:15-16

Perhaps our Creator imagined all that he would do before he actually began to speak it into being. We were a product of his imagination. Consider what the world would be like without the dreamers, the ones who imagine things that are not yet, but could be. From art to music to medicine, we are the beneficiaries of someone's intense desire to create, someone's ability to imagine a brighter future or a better way of doing things.

This week share your gratitude, not only for those who have brought us a better world, or for God, who imagined every detail of every living thing, but for your own ability to imagine good things. From your imagination comes the inspiration to move forward and to dream bigger dreams. God gave us each a little part of himself in the gift of imagination.

Let the child inside you come out to play. Give that child room to create in a new way, to envision some untried possibility with full confidence that it can happen. Keep your imagination strong and vivid. It pleases God when you do.

I am enough of an artist to draw freely upon my imagination. Imagination is more important than knowledge. Knowledge is limited. Imagination encircles the world.
—Albert Einstein

Lord, thank you for all that you have imagined for my life…

WEEK 34/ DAY 2: *Creatively Me!*

*I perceived that there was nothing better for human beings but to
enjoy what they do because that's what they're allotted in life.*
—Ecclesiastes 3:22

It's good to enjoy not only what you do, but how you do it. This week try to imagine new ways to do what you do. What can you add to your day that will make it more fun or more creative? What can you do to stretch your thinking until you discover a new possibility or opportunity? As a creative human being, you can go as far as your imagination will take you.

Our imagination is the only limit to what we can hope to have in the future.
—Charles F. Kettering

Lord, thank you for giving me the gift of imagination ...

WEEK 34/ DAY 3: *Heavenly Aspirations*

*Greatness and grandeur are in front of him; / strength and
beauty are in his sanctuary.* —Psalm 96:6

When God imagined earth and the universe that we know, he also imagined vast universes beyond our own. He even imagined a place where he would reside and where we can go when we return to him. He gave us aspirations toward heaven. He reminded us that there's more to life and more to our souls than we understand. All we have to do is trust him and imagine what it will be like to one day be with him.

*Heaven will be the perfection we have always longed for. All the things that made
Earth unlovely and tragic will be absent in Heaven.* —Billy Graham

Lord, though I can't always imagine what heaven will be like, I love thinking about being with you one day ...

WEEK 34/ DAY 4: *The Future Is So Bright!*

Stop worrying about tomorrow, because tomorrow will worry about itself. Each day has enough trouble of its own.
—Matthew 6:34

Whatever the day brings, we know that we only have this moment, this present opportunity. With that, we have the option to imagine a future that might be different from what we experience in life right now. We have a chance to put our hopes and desires in front of our heavenly Father, who will brighten each step of the way.

The future is as bright as the promises of God. —Adoniram Judson

Lord, I can't always imagine my bright future, but I'm glad you can…

WEEK 34/ DAY 5: *Imagining a Peaceful World*

Happy are people who make peace, because they will be called God's children. —Matthew 5:9

It's important to imagine peace, because when we do, we help to create peace. We cannot achieve something we cannot perceive or imagine. As you go through the week, consider all the ways that you can bring the spirit of peace to anything you do.

Keep your heart in peace; let nothing in the world disturb it: everything has an end.
—John of the Cross

Lord, help me believe and trust in your peace and thank you…

WEEK 34/ DAY 6: *Dreaming of You*

This is my commandment: love each other just as I have loved you. —John 15:12

Imagine what it means to truly love others! Perhaps you dreamed or even still dream of finding the right partner to share your life, or perhaps you hoped and prayed for the right kind of friend to talk with about your interests and ideas. Perhaps you still dream about love in any of its forms. Thank God for imagining what our hearts would value when it comes to love.

It is by loving and being loved that one can come nearest to the soul of another. —George MacDonald

Lord, thank you for imagining love that fills the heart…

WEEK 34/ DAY 7: *Giving and Getting*

In everything I have shown you that, by working hard, we must help the weak. In this way we remember the Lord Jesus' words: "It is more blessed to give than to receive." —Acts 20:35

Life is more about giving than getting. God wants you to get what you need and then give from your abundance to those around you. God made you a generous person so that you could enjoy his gifts and share them with your neighbors. Each day brings a new lesson in giving.

Find out how much God has given you and take from it what you need; the remainder is needed by others. —Augustine of Hippo

Lord, you are so generous to me. Thank you for giving me more than I need…

Thankful for Discipline

No discipline is fun while it lasts, but it seems painful at the time. Later, however, it yields the peaceful fruit of righteousness for those who have been trained by it.
—Hebrews 12:11

It doesn't necessarily feel good when God sends you to your room to think things over and examine your heart. He does it not make you miserable, but to make you marvelous. He does it because he knows that you are one of his most beloved beings and he wants everything to bring you closer to him. You are disciplined as a measure of helping you see more clearly what God wants from you. His discipline is not quite the same as that of an earthly parent, because he knows everything about you and he knows you inside and out, more than you may know yourself.

Because he knows you so well, God believes in you and trusts you to strive to become all he imagined you to be when he created you. You're the work of his hands and a masterpiece at that and so it is his great pleasure to guide you and teach you. He does not discipline you to punish you or to discourage you, but does so to enlighten you and help you find your way. Thank him for loving you enough to care for you with discipline.

The goal of God's discipline is restoration—never condemnation.
—Author unknown

Lord, thank you for bringing things to my attention that I need to work on and change…

WEEK 35/ DAY 2: *Healthy Habits*

He lets me rest in grassy meadows; / he leads me to restful waters;
/ he keeps me alive. —Psalm 23:2-3

It's not easy to form a habit that offers you a balance between work and play, rest and activity. God designed you to work, but also to rest and to breathe in the beauty around you. Thank him for restful moments and for guiding you into good habits that keep you healthy.

Early to bed and early to rise, / Helps make you healthy, wealthy, and wise.
—Benjamin Franklin (adapted)

Lord, thank you for guiding me to take better care of my restful times and for my health…

WEEK 35/ DAY 3: *Prayer Posture*

Stay alert and pray so that you won't give in to temptation. The
spirit is eager, but the flesh is weak. —Matthew 26:41

Prayer takes a special kind of discipline even for those who are well practiced at doing it regularly. It's easy to give in to being too busy or too tired or too moody to respond the nudge of your spirit to simply stop everything and pray. Thankfully, the spirit persists and helps us to develop a great prayer posture.

It is possible to offer fervent prayer even while walking in public or strolling alone, or
seated in your shop while buying or selling—or even while cooking.
—John Chrysostom

Lord, thank you that I can pray on my knees or on the fly and that you always welcome the words of my heart…

WEEK 35/ DAY 4: *Money, Money, Money*

People who are trying to get rich fall into temptation. They are trapped by many stupid and harmful passions that plunge people into ruin and destruction. The love of money is the root of all kinds of evil. —1 Timothy 6:9-10

Money requires a lot of discipline both in the saving and the spending of it. More important than whether you have a large bank account, though, is to discipline your heart in matters of money. Try to discover what place money has in your life. Do you serve money, or does money serve you?

Money is always either our master or our slave. —Latin proverb

Lord, thank you for working with me in areas of money...

WEEK 35/ DAY 5: *Read and Study*

Aim to live quietly, mind your own business, and earn your own living, just as I told you. —1 Thessalonians 4:11

God designed you to have communion with him in a variety of ways. He wants you to freely come to him in prayer, to learn from his Word, and to live in a way that brings you both joy. Those quiet moments spent with him each day provide nourishment like nothing else can.

There are three stages of Bible reading: (1) the cod liver stage, when you take it like medicine; (2) the shredded wheat stage when it's nourishing but dry; (3) the peaches and cream stage when it's consumed with passion and pleasure. —Author unknown

Lord, thank you for your Word and for disciplining me in my reading and quiet time...

WEEK 35/ DAY 6: *Drawing Closer to God*

Yes, the LORD definitely disciplined me, but he didn't hand me over to death. —Psalm 118:18

God loves you so much that he always wants to be close to you. Any time you choose to nestle into his arm or sit at his feet, you both thrive. Your relationship with him matters more than anything you could ever aspire to accomplish.

Thank him for giving you some sweetly godly ways. Godliness is glory in the seed, and glory is godliness in the flower. —William Gurnall

Lord, thank you for your generous spirit that disciplines me into more godly ways…

❦

WEEK 35/ DAY 7: *Routines, Rules, and Ruts*

So, all of us who are spiritually mature should think this way and if anyone thinks differently, God will reveal it to him or her. Only let's live in a way that is consistent with whatever level we have reached. —Philippians 3:15-16

Obeying God is certainly a measure of our discipline. You may establish a routine where you connect with him every morning at dawn or every evening at bedtime. You may play by all the rules. The best part of your discipline, however, will be the one of keeping your heart fully engaged any time you're near him. That's how you stay out of the ruts.

The perpetual hurry of business and company ruins me in soul if not in body. —William Wilberforce

Lord, thank you for our connection and for your willingness to be near me any time at all…

Thankful for Gifts

I am the vine; you are the branches. If you remain in me and I in you, then you will produce much fruit. Without me, you can't do anything.
—*John 15:5*

How blessed and wonderful, beloved, are the gifts of God. Life in immortality, splendor in righteousness, truth in perfect confidence, faith in assurance, self-control in holiness!"

This statement from the First Epistle of Clement reminds us of the fact that everything we have in this life is a gift from God. The fact that our souls are eternal because of the gift of Jesus Christ is essential to all that we are. The opportunity we have to grow in spirit and truth because of God's Word is a gift.

Who you are, your talents, your virtues and vices, your outward beauty and inward soul, are gifts from your Maker, the One who sees you as worthy at all times to receive his gifts so that you can live abundantly. If your heart overflows with gratitude for all that you have and all that you are, it is indeed the right attitude and position to take. God is the vine. Everything else comes from being grafted on to his Spirit. Everything else comes from his nourishing love and grace. How blessed we are indeed to have his wonderful gifts!

For every created being whatsoever that is endowed with power, whether of healing or the like, possesses it not of itself, but as a thing given it by God.
—Cyril of Alexandria

Lord, giver of life and all that is, I thank you for the gifts you've given me…

WEEK 36/ DAY 2: *The Gift of Today*

Give us the bread we need for today. —Matthew 6:11

Sometimes you can get so caught up with the worries and concerns of tomorrow you forget to enjoy today. You forget that today is also a gift and that it will not get a repeat performance. You won't get to do this day ever again. God gives you the bread of life to nourish you each day, one meal at a time.

He who gives you the day will also give you the things necessary for the day.
—Gregory of Nyssa

Lord, it is with gratitude and joy I come before you today…

WEEK 36/ DAY 3: *The Gift of Grace*

God has given his grace to each one of us measured out by the gift that is given by Christ. —Ephesians 4:7

Imagine a day without living in grace. Try to picture what it would be like if every mistake, every sin, every fleeting horrific thought were recorded and held against you. The God of the universe knows that you could not bear up under that kind of sorrow even for a day and so he has chosen to cover you, every day and every moment by grace.

Your worst days are never so bad that you are beyond the reach of God's grace. And your best days are never so good that you are beyond the need of God's grace.
—Jerry Bridges

Lord, I celebrate your loving-kindness and grace…

WEEK 36/ DAY 4: *The Gift of Faith*

You are saved by God's grace because of your faith. This salvation is God's gift. It's not something you possessed. It's not something you did that you can be proud of. Instead, we are God's accomplishment. —Ephesians 2:8-10

If you treat your faith like a glorious gift, holding it up, studying it, enjoying it, and sharing it with others because of its infinite beauty, then you will be living your faith every day. You will not lose sight of how precious this gift to you really is.

When we have an atom of faith in our hearts, we can see God's face, gentle, serene and approving. —John Calvin

Lord, I thank you for the faith I have in you …

WEEK 36/ DAY 5: *The Gift of Forgiveness*

This is why I tell you that her many sins have been forgiven; so she has shown great love. The one who is forgiven little loves little. —Luke 7:47

If you can count your sins on one hand, chances are you may not actually appreciate what it means that God forgives you of your sins. If it takes both hands, and all your toes, you're getting closer. When you stop to consider all you've done that requires God's reasonable and forgiving heart, the more you come to love him for his gift of forgiveness.

Forgiveness is the answer to the child's dream of a miracle by which what is broken is made whole again, what is soiled is again made clean. —Dag Hammarskjöld

Lord, how can I begin to thank you for all that you've done to offer me forgiveness and blessing? …

WEEK 36/ DAY 6: *The Gift of Friendship*

*I call you friends, because everything I heard from my Father I
have made known to you. You didn't choose me, but I chose you.*
—John 15:15-16

You have friends. You have close friends who know you well and share life's
ups and downs, its grief and joys. You have friends at work or at church, those
you rely on in other ways that you don't hold as closely to your heart. You have
a friend in Jesus, the most amazing friend you could ever have. His love makes
you a gift to others.

A faithful friend is an image of God. —French proverb

Lord, my heart is full of love because of your friendship, and so I thank
you…

WEEK 36/ DAY 7: *The Gift of Happiness*

*All the days of the needy are hard, but a happy heart has a
continual feast.* —Proverbs 15:15

Sometimes it feels as if the world is suffering from a massive depression. It's
hard to find the people of joy. As a person tied to the heart of God, though, you
have every reason to be happy. Spread the joy you know everywhere you go.

There is no happiness in having or in getting, but only in giving.
—Henry Drummond

Lord, thank you for giving me a glad heart…

Thankful for Memories

Remember the days long past; consider the years long gone.
—Deuteronomy 32:7

Wherever you are today, your heart and mind are filled with thousands of images, some distant, some sharp and clear, about experiences and places and people that have shaped your life. You have childhood memories of growing up in a certain house or neighborhood, going to a particular school, or being friends with someone special. You remember the best of those times, and sometimes even the worst of those times.

Then as you grew into a mature adult, your memories became filled with searches for the right partner to share your life, the right work to engage your talents, and the right places to live and explore. You became more aware of the world at large and your scrapbook overflowed with all that you created.

As you continue to grow and change and become more of the person God intended, your heartfelt memories will become legacies. They will be the pieces of your life mosaic that remind you of all you've accomplished and attempted. They'll be the picture God carries in his wallet of you and your family. How proud he is of you! Thank him every day for the beautiful memories you've already collected, for there are more to come!

Things that were hard to bear are sweet to remember. —Seneca

Lord, thank you for those memories that touch my heart again and again with joy…

WEEK 37/ DAY 2: *Once Upon a Time*

When I was a child, I used to speak like a child, reason like a child, think like a child. But now that I have become a man, I've put an end to childish things. —1 Corinthians 13:11

It may seem like some long-lost fairy tale to think back about your childhood. No matter what it was really like, in your heart's memory it takes on shadowy moments of triumph and discovery. It is the place where you first became aware of who you are. It helped to plant the seeds of your life today.

The greatest poem ever known / is one all poets have outgrown:/ The poetry, innate, untold, / of being only four years old. —Christopher Morley, "To a Child"

Lord, what joy it is to have warm childhood memories…

WEEK 37/ DAY 3: *A Little Life Experience*

The memory of the righteous is a blessing. —Proverbs 10:7

You experience life in numerous ways. You touch it and taste it, smell it and see it, and you feel it in every fiber of your being. Once you've had the experience of it, it stays with you, lingering long past the moment, holding you close so that the experience can guide you on your way. Thank God for the experiences he brings to you.

The trouble with learning from experience is that you never graduate. —Author unknown

Lord, I praise you for the wonder and joy of life and all that I experience…

WEEK 37 / DAY 4: *Memories of Love*

Rushing waters can't quench love; rivers can't wash it away.
—Song of Songs 8:7

Memory serves to keep love fresh and new. It protects it somewhere close to your heart so that whether your thoughts wander to the love you feel for your children, the love of your spouse, or the love of a dear friend, nothing can erase such beautiful experiences of love. Hallelujah!

People are renewed by love. As sinful desire ages them, so love rejuvenates them.
—Augustine of Hippo

Lord, thank you for the tender and loving memories that cling to my heart…

WEEK 37 / DAY 5: *Spirit Nudges*

God is the one who establishes us with you in Christ and who anointed us. God also sealed us and gave the Spirit as a down payment in our hearts. —2 Corinthians 1:21-22

Just as God nudged Paul all those centuries ago, he nudges at your heart today. He sealed you and gave you his Spirit because he wanted you to remember him in all that you do. His Spirit washes over you to make you aware that God is always near.

The renewal of our natures is a work of great importance. It is not to be done in a day. We have not only a new house to build up, but an old one to pull down.
—George Whitefield

Lord, thank you that your Spirit nudges my heart…

WEEK 37/ DAY 6: *A Sense of Belonging*

So now you are no longer strangers and aliens. Rather, you are fellow citizens with God's people, and you belong to God's household. —Ephesians 2:19

You've been encountering God in the community of believers for a long time. What joy it is to recall the memories of those you've prayed with and studied with, those who are part of your family in Christ. Memories of moments together belong to you forever.

And ye shall gather yourselves together frequently, seeking what is fitting for your souls. —Didache

Lord, what warm memories fill my heart of those who have walked the way with me…

WEEK 37/ DAY 7: *Bountiful Blessings*

The LORD bless you and keep you. / The LORD make his face shine on you and be gracious to you. / The LORD lift up his face to you and grant you peace. —Numbers 6:24-26

Recalling your blessings lets you live them over and over again. Each time your heart fills with gratitude for all God has done, rejoice. Your memories of his goodness and his kindness and his grace keep you close to his heart and keep your heart close to him.

What a world this would be if we could forget our troubles as easily as we forget our blessings. —Author unknown

Lord, I know I cannot begin to count my blessings, and my heart is grateful…

Thankful for Hard Work

❧

Whatever you do, do it from the heart for the Lord and not for people.
　　　　　　—Colossians 3:23

Even if we complain slightly when it feels like we have too much work to do, or when we've had to work hard to create something new, the truth is that we are at our best when we work, and especially so when we work hard. This week, we'll give God the glory for all those things that cause you to go the distance, make you walk the extra mile, and give you an adrenalin rush. It's when you have to push yourself to become more, to do more, to keep making the effort, that you learn how strong you are.

God loves to see you put maximum effort into creating your dreams, raising your children, or building a relationship. All those things take work, and when you offer thanks and praise for each of those opportunities, you have an even better chance for great success.

Imagine what it means to give all you've got to the work in front of you this week. Andrew Carnegie said, "The average person puts only 25% of his energy and ability into his work. The world takes off its hat to those who put in more than 50% of their capacity, and stands on its head for those few and far between souls who devote 100%."

What will you give this week? Thank God for every chance you have to work hard at your task, to focus on great possibility, and to give 100%. You can awe the world!

The harder you work, the harder it is to surrender. —Vince Lombardi

Lord, thank you for giving me a chance to shine …

WEEK 38/ DAY 2: *Don't Quit Your Day Job!*

Workers deserve their pay. —Luke 10:7

If you've ever lost a job, been down-sized, right-sized, or ostracized, you know what it means to not have work to do. You know that it's hard to overcome the financial decline and the lowered self-esteem. In those moments, you would do almost anything to be working again. You're ready to give the next job all you've got.

On the other hand, you might have a job that is no longer meaningful to you, or one that feels like you've got nowhere to go. It may be tempting then to slack off and give it less than your best effort. Whatever your situation is, you're called to do your work with gratitude and to make every effort to shine. Sometimes, that's hard work.

I find that the harder I work, the more luck I seem to have. —Thomas Jefferson

Lord, I appreciate my job and I thank you for the work I do…

WEEK 38/ DAY 3: *Stretching and Bending*

While physical training has some value, training in holy living is useful for everything. —1 Timothy 4:8

Working out and exercising on a regular basis is valuable. Often, it's hard work because it requires discipline, especially when you're tired or simply not in the mood to have to do it one more time. The fact remains that you reward yourself every time you choose the workout, though. God rewards you, too, every time you are intentional about stretching and bending to reach your goals, both physical and spiritual.

The secret of success is constancy of purpose. —Benjamin Disraeli

Lord, thank you for helping me stick to the work I need to do…

WEEK 38/ DAY 4: *Love Is Work!*

Set me as a seal over your heart, / as a seal upon your arm, / for love is as strong as death. —Song of Songs 8:6

No two people ever entered into a relationship that wasn't work. Whether they were friends or lovers, siblings or family, securing the bond between them took energy from them both. Your relationship with God takes work, on your part and on His. The beauty of it all is that your hard work pays off because your love grows and flourishes when you commit to it with your whole heart.

In labors of love, every day is payday. —Gaines Brewster

Lord, I understand that love is a lot of work, but no work fills me more with gratitude…

WEEK 38/ DAY 5: *Working Out Your Salvation*

Carry out your own salvation with fear and trembling. God is the one who enables you both to want and to actually live out his good purposes. —Philippians 2:12-13

You may not see yourself as working out your own salvation, but in a sense, you are called to do so. God invited you into his presence and offered you his gift of grace, but each day, you can choose to live fully in his presence or you can stand aside, going your own way, suffering alone, until you turn again to him. Thank God he is always there to receive you.

A world of nice people, content in their own niceness, looking no further, turned away from God, would be just as desperately in need of salvation as a miserable world—and might even be more difficult to save. —C. S. Lewis

Lord, thank you for always being there for me…

WEEK 38/ DAY 6: *The Trouble with Trouble*

We even take pride in our problems, because we know that trouble produces endurance, endurance produces character, and character produces hope. —Romans 5:3-4

The trouble with trouble is that it too is a lot of work. You have to fret about it and worry a lot. You have to talk about it and share your woes. You have to wonder if God hears your prayers, and finally you have to deal with it and move on. You have to endure it and find the hope. The good news about trouble is that it gives you every reason to hope.

God will not look you over for medals, degrees or diplomas, but for scars. —Author unknown

Lord, thank you for being with me any time I've had troubles to share…

WEEK 38/ DAY 7: *Hard Lessons*

There's no end to the excessive production of scrolls. Studying too much wearies the body. —Ecclesiastes 12:12

As a student of life, you've had your share of hard lessons. In fact, you may go through times when you wonder if you're the only one who has to learn one more lesson by the hand of God. After all, doesn't he have other students? When life is hard and the lessons are long, thank God that he is closer to you than ever.

Learning is not a spectator sport. —Author unknown

Lord, it seems that I've always got another hard lesson to learn, but I thank you that I don't have to learn it all by myself…

Thankful for Forgiveness

⌘

Happy are those whose sin isn't counted against them by the Lord.
—Romans 4:8

Imagine what your life would look like or feel like if God did not forgive your sins. His forgiveness gives you the opportunity to change and to grow and to live freely. His forgiveness is one of the greatest attributes of healing that your body and soul can experience. Even more so is the understanding that his forgiveness helps to link your spirit from this world into the next.

All of us need to be forgiven sometimes, and we're grateful that we have a God who loves us so much that he brings us fully back to himself by forgiving the things we do so thoughtlessly. "Forgive us our debts as we forgive our debtors," we pray often. As we focus on the beauty and healing power of forgiveness, let's give praise and thanks to God and to those people in our lives who have been willing to forgive us for wrongs and who help guide us into right living. God is faithful to forgive when our hearts humbly seek him.

Dear Lord and Father of mankind, / forgive our foolish ways; reclothe us in our rightful mind, / in purer lives thy service find, / in deeper reverence, praise.
—John Greenleaf Whittier

Lord, I am brought to my knees with gratitude for your gift of forgiveness...

WEEK 39/ DAY 2: *Forgive Yourself*

All the prophets testify about him that everyone who believes in him receives forgiveness of sins through his name. —Acts 10:43

Thank God for your humanness, your weakness, even those things you may regret from days gone by. Thank him that he loves you so much, he no longer wants you to bear the burden of carrying those sins around with you. He put them all at the cross to free your arms for praise and your heart for joy. Forgive yourself! God already has!

The moment an individual can accept and forgive himself, even a little, is the moment in which he becomes to some degree lovable. —Eugene Kennedy

Lord, thank you for loving me as I am and forgiving me…

WEEK 39/ DAY 3: *Forgive Others*

Be tolerant with each other and, if someone has a complaint against anyone, forgive each other. As the Lord forgave you, so also forgive each other. —Colossians 3:13

Think about each person this week who still holds a part of you simply because you haven't closed the door on old wounds. As you recall the wound, take a step closer to the person who wounded you and offer a truce. Lay the burden down and thank God it is finally over. You can be at peace each time your heart gives way to forgiveness. Give God the glory!

He who forgives ends the quarrel. —Author unknown

Lord, thank you for helping me forgive…

WEEK 39/ DAY 4: *Forgive Your Parents*

The glory of children is their parents. —Proverbs 17:6

You may not hold any conscious grudges against your parents or your upbringing, but somewhere along the way, you may have experienced tremendous disappointment with them. The beautiful thing about forgiveness, though, is that it gives you new eyes to see and a new heart to understand and let go. Forgiveness changes your view.

When you forgive, you in no way change the past—but you sure do change the future. —Bernard Meltzer

Lord, thank you for my parents...

WEEK 39/ DAY 5: *Forgive Your Circumstances*

Be angry without sinning. Don't let the sun set on your anger.
Don't provide an opportunity for the devil.
—Ephesians 4:26-27

Do you ever have days when you look around and wonder how you got where you are? What happened that your life is in the midst of a whirlpool of swirling problems, a seemingly never-ending downward spiral? Stop the spinning and churning and step closer to God. Forgive your surroundings and seek the path God truly has designed for you.

Forgiveness is the fragrance the violet sheds on the heel that has crushed it.
—Mark Twain

Lord, I confess I don't understand my life situation, but I thank you for staying close to me...

WEEK 39/ DAY 6: *Forgive Your Body*

Forgive, and you will be forgiven. Give, and it will be given to you.
A good portion—packed down, firmly shaken, and overflow-
ing—will fall into your lap. —Luke 6:37-38

Your body is a gift to you; it's the sanctuary where your soul lives and your heart rules. It's the place where you meet others and live life. It's also the vehicle that may cause you sorrow if it becomes ill or depressed. It may cause you to wonder that you weren't somehow designed in a different way. Forgive your body if you hold any resentment toward it and be free.

To carry a grudge is like being stung to death by one bee. —William H. Walton

Lord, I admit that I get frustrated with my body, but I thank you...

WEEK 39/ DAY 7: *Forgive Love*

The one who is forgiven little loves little. —Luke 7:47

Love toots its horn and blows a lot of smoke and sometimes breaks your heart. It can do a number on your spirit and deprive you of inner peace. At least, it can do that when it seems to all go haywire. When love doesn't serve you in the way you thought it would, then let it go and forgive the pain it caused. When you do, you'll find it shifts and changes to bring you back to joy.

Love is an act of faith, and whoever is of little faith is also of little love.
—Erich Fromm

Lord, I am grateful for love, even when it has not always gone my way...

Thankful for Music

By day the LORD *commands his faithful love; / by night his song is with me.*
    —*Psalm 42:8*

If marching bands could no longer beat their drums and sound the bugles that draw our attention, or if symphonies could no longer play the heart-wrenching melodies that transport us into other dimensions, or if rock and roll had never hit the music scene, the world might seem colorless and melancholy. Fortunately, the God of the universe gave us ears to hear the rhythms of incredible sounds from songbirds to divas. He filled our spirits with a desire and a need to worship him with music and praise.

Music strikes a chord in your heart every time you hear the National Anthem or the Wedding March or the call to worship. It sets your feet to tapping and your hands to clapping and your life to joy. Thank God that he always has a song to fill your heart. You have every reason to lift up your voice to him. In fact, it's a good time to turn up the volume!

God has preached the gospel through music. —Martin Luther

Lord, I know I've got the music in me, and I thank you…

WEEK 40/ DAY 2: *With Thanks and Praise*

Praise the LORD! / Sing to the LORD a new song; / sing God's praise in the assembly of the faithful! —Psalm 149:1

Nothing is quite as beautiful to the Lord as the sound of his people's voices raised up to him in praise and worship. He loves to hear you sing no matter how good your voice might be. He'll never reject you from the choir, because you're one of his favorite singers. Thank God for your voice and let him hear you sing!

One day all Christians will join in a doxology and sing God's praises with perfection. But even today, individually and corporately, we are not only to sing the doxology, but to be the doxology. —Francis Schaeffer

Lord, I thank you for putting me in the choir…

WEEK 40/ DAY 3: *The Beat Goes On!*

Let every living thing praise the LORD! —Psalm 150:6

Do you hear it? The rhythm of life hums through you, resonating with your spirit and lifting your heart up in great joy. It slows down with the beat of change, quickening as it reaches a new bend in the road and whispering a new song. You're part of the music of life, part of all that makes the world echo in beautiful and rich harmony.

Life is a symphony and at various times you either conduct the orchestra, or sit in the first chair, or you take your place in the audience. In any case, you're always a part of the music. —Karen Moore

Lord, thank you that I am part of the music of life…

WEEK 40/ DAY 4: *Just Humming Along*

Although your former state was ordinary, your future will be extraordinary. —Job 8:7

Some days you may not hear the music, you may simply be humming along, doing what you must do, living and working and giving what you can. Other days, the music is almost deafening in its appeal to you, its desire to strengthen and renew you. Humming is good for a time because it keeps you in step with the music, waiting patiently, until it's time to dance again!

God aims to exalt himself by working for those who wait for him. —John Piper

Lord, thank you for keeping me humming along…

WEEK 40/ DAY 5: *Of Crickets, Birds, and Other Glorious Singers!*

Look at the birds in the sky. They don't sow seed or harvest grain or gather crops into barns. Yet your heavenly Father feeds them. —Matthew 6:26

There's something wonderful about a quiet summer night, crickets chirping away in the grass, frogs lifting their voices to the heavens, and owls giving an occasional hoot just for fun. The birds of the air and the creatures of the planet all know that they can sing because they trust everything to the Creator. They know he is the only conductor of the orchestra of life.

Good morning, theologians! You wake and sing. But I, old fool, know less than you and worry over everything, instead of simply trusting in the heavenly Father's care. —Martin Luther (to the birds as he walked in the woods)

Lord, thank you that I can trust in you for everything…

WEEK 40/ DAY 6: *On Harmony and Discord*

When a person's path draws favor from the LORD, even their enemies are at peace with them. —Proverbs 16:7

Those ups and downs of life can create such chaos that sometimes we can't hear the simple strains of peace that God is trying to offer. When that happens, it's important to step back, quiet your spirit, and then listen with your heart. God wants your life to be one of peace and harmony. It's up to you to tune him in more clearly.

God never ceases to speak to us, but the noise of the world without and the tumult of our passions within bewilder us and prevent us from listening to him.
—François Fénelon

Lord, I thank you for the days of harmony you bring…

WEEK 40/ DAY 7: *When the Saints Go Marching In*

Because for me, living serves Christ and dying is even better.
—Philippians 1:21

One thing about the music is that it continues to play throughout this life and the next. Whether we go into heaven with a marching band or simply hear the welcoming chorus of angels, we trust that God is always in control. Our lives are meant to get us through the dance, preparing to sing with all those who have gone before us. It's a chorus of love!

Music, the greatest good that mortals know, / And all of heaven we have below.
—Joseph Addison

Lord, thank you for keeping me in tune with you…

Thankful for Books!

Oh, that my words were written down, / inscribed on a scroll /
with an iron instrument and lead, / forever engraved on stone.
—Job 19:23

God must have known we'd have a great love for books and for learning since he inspired a number of authors to create the Scriptures. Of course, that book has been the most popular book of all time and continues to speak to us and guide us.

Books are vehicles that carry us away, transporting us to places we might never travel or giving us insight into the lives of others that we would never experience. Books teach us how to make things and how to create gourmet delights. They teach us how to handle difficult situations and how to build our businesses. Books are a refuge for the spirit and a discipline for our minds.

God uses tools of every sort to shape and mold us, and books are one of his greatest resources. Even with the resources available to us on the internet these days, most of us wouldn't give up the chance to slip quietly away into a cozy corner of the room and enjoy pleasant hours with our favorite authors. Ideas to ponder, dreams to pursue, insights to gain, infinite treasures await us in the simple pages of books.

Thank God! A good book is the precious life-blood of a master-spirit, embalmed and treasured up on purpose to a life beyond life. —John Milton

Lord, I thank you for the treasures I discover in books…

WEEK 41 / DAY 2: *Quiet Time*

If not, you must hear me; be quiet, and I will teach you wisdom.
—Job 33:33

There's almost nothing more soothing to your spirit than taking a little time away from the world, perhaps to read or to pray or to contemplate life or the things of God. Often, a book will bring an opportunity to rest and be quiet, things that make your heart eternally grateful.

Everywhere I have sought rest and not found it, except sitting in a corner by myself with a little book. —Thomas à Kempis

Lord, thank you for those precious moments when I can just be quiet…

WEEK 41 / DAY 3: *Read to Me*

Pay attention to my words. / Bend your ear to my speech. / Don't let them slip from your sight. / Guard them in your mind.
—Proverbs 4:20-21

Do you remember how much you enjoyed being read to when you were a child? Perhaps it was bedtime and your mom read you a story, or your teacher made sure you were exposed to some of the great literature of our times. Maybe you like to read to someone else. Be thankful anytime you get to read to someone or when someone shares a book with you.

Seek in reading and you will find in meditation; knock in prayer and it will be opened to you in contemplation. —John of the Cross

Lord, there's nothing more wonderful than reading a book aloud…

WEEK 41 / DAY 4: *Reading and Understanding*

Running up to the carriage, Philip heard the man reading the prophet Isaiah. He asked, "Do you really understand what you are reading?" —Acts 8:30

We're all students. No matter what age or stage we are in life, we continue to learn things and to try to understand things. We may have numerous resources, but the gift of the Holy Spirit is to offer us help in gaining wisdom and understanding. Invite the Holy Spirit into your studies, into your reading life.

The delight of opening a new pursuit, or a new course of reading, imparts the vivacity and novelty of youth even to old age. —Benjamin Disraeli

Lord, thank you for giving me so many precious tools for learning...

WEEK 41 / DAY 5: *Of Authors and Writers*

Now go, write it before them on a tablet, / inscribe it on a scroll, / so in the future it will endure as a witness. —Isaiah 30:8

Writers are people who have a need to express themselves. Authors are people who want to inspire, teach, impress, please, or experience more of life through and with their readers. Thankfully, writers and authors give us a continual stream of beautiful and provocative works.

The most original authors are not so because they advance what is new, but because they put what they have to say as if it had never been said before. —Goethe

Lord, I am grateful for those who write...

WEEK 41 / DAY 6: *Of Generous Genres*

Teach the wise, and they will become wiser; / inform the righteous, and their learning will increase. —Proverbs 9:9

Are you overwhelmed when you walk into a big bookstore and scan the shelves? There are infinite possibilities for topics and materials to draw your attention. It can be difficult to even choose what area of interest you most want to engage in. Books abound and how blessed we are to have such easy access to the printed word.

The two most engaging powers of an author are to make new things familiar and familiar things new. —William Makepeace Thackeray

Lord, thank you for those writers who continue to make things new for me…

WEEK 41 / DAY 7: *Life Lessons*

The days of a human life are like grass: / they bloom like a wildflower; / but when the wind blows through it, it's gone.
—Psalm 103:15

To be sure, life is a quickly fleeing opportunity and it's up to us to make choices that bring us greater possibility for fulfillment and joy. God has blessed us with books to enjoy, to learn from, and to help us when we're in the midst of another lesson, another experience somewhat out of our comfort zone.

The law of God and also the way of life is written in our hearts; it lies in no man's supposing, nor in any historical opinion, but in a good will and well doing.
—Jacob Böhme

Lord, I'm always going through some kind of life lesson, so I thank you for those who write books that help me find my way…

Thankful for Miracles

❧

Jesus did many other things as well. If all of them were recorded, I imagine the world itself wouldn't have enough room for the scrolls that would be written.
—John 21:25

What does it take for you to consider something to be a miracle? Does it have to defy the laws of nature, or be demonstrated in a way that everyone else can see the miracle too? Perhaps everything is a miracle. The fact that you can think for yourself, walk on two feet, love with a full heart, and imagine more possibility than you currently see, perhaps all those things are miracles.

Most of us think of babies as miracles or of healings for those who have been extremely ill. We think of the miracles of Jesus as he healed the lepers and as he raised Lazarus from the dead. Certainly, walking on the water as Jesus did to meet the disciples in a boat, was some kind of miracle.

Focus on the miracles in your life this week and see how astounding the God of the universe can be. You worship a supernatural God who does incredible things!

Miracles are not contrary to nature, but only contrary to what we know about nature. —Augustine of Hippo

Lord, thank you for the miracles you perform even today…

WEEK 42/ DAY 2: *Of Answered Prayers*

I prayed for this boy, and the LORD gave me what I asked from him. —1 Samuel 1:27

You've had amazing answers to prayer and in your heart of hearts, you know that they were true gifts from God, little miracles of his love for you. They may not have been big supernatural events that stopped the world, but they were showers of rain on your parched spirit, or blossoms of joy when things seemed lackluster and gray. God loves to hear and answer your prayers.

When you can't put your prayers into words, God hears your heart.
—Author unknown

Lord, I thank you for the little miracles you offer me through prayer...

WEEK 42/ DAY 3: *Of Unanswered Prayers*

Keep on praying and guard your prayers with thanksgiving.
—Colossians 4:2

Perhaps miracles occur even when we don't realize it at the time. Those may come to us by God's grace in the form of prayers that don't go as we had hoped and that seemingly go unanswered. The fact is, they were answered in a way that was actually better for us. They were miracles of grace that caused us to move in a new direction.

I have had prayers answered—most strangely so sometimes—but I think our heavenly Father's loving-kindness has been even more evident in what He has refused me. —Lewis Carroll

Lord, thank you for knowing what is best for me all the time; that in itself is a miracle...

WEEK 42/ DAY 4: *Healing Hearts, Minds, and Bodies*

I will seek out the lost, bring back the strays, bind up the wounded, and strengthen the weak. —Ezekiel 34:16

God is in the miracle business. He takes our broken hearts, our weak minds, and our ailing bodies and makes them whole again. That's his commitment to us as our loving Father. He wants us to live fully and well. Thank him for the continual blessing that only he can truly give to all that makes you whole.

As for me, I know of nothing but miracles. —Walt Whitman

Lord, I live in gratitude for the miracle of your grace and mercy…

WEEK 42/ DAY 5: *Of Timing, Fate, and God's Planning*

God has prepared things for those who love him that no eye has seen, or ear has heard, or that haven't crossed the mind of any human being. God has revealed these things to us through the Spirit. —1 Corinthians 2:9-10

You may think you were just in the right place at the right time, or that fate intervened to give you the right partner or the right job, but the truth is more miracle than fate, more gift than coincidence. God has been planning the details of your life since you took your first breath. After all, you're one of his miracles.

Providence has at all times been my only dependence, for all other resources seem to have failed us. —George Washington

Lord, I thank you for remembering me and creating opportunities…

WEEK 42/ DAY 6: *Of Sunsets and Stardust*

What came into being through the Word was life, / and the life was the light for all people. / The light shines in the darkness, / and the darkness doesn't extinguish the light. —John 1:3-5

When you chance upon a bright red sunset or the appearance of a big, round, coppery moon, you can't help feeling God's presence. You can't help realizing the miracles that this planet holds. From the stars to the ocean depths, miracles abound, all treasures from our loving Lord.

Two things fill me with constantly increasing admiration and awe, the longer and more earnestly I reflect on them: the starry heavens without and the moral law within. —Immanuel Kant

Lord, you have given us an amazing home, full of the miracles of life…

WEEK 42/ DAY 7: *Of the Holy Spirit*

We haven't received the world's spirit but God's Spirit so that we can know the things given to us by God. —1 Corinthians 2:12

Isn't it awesome to realize that you can understand the things of God because of his willingness to put his remarkable and loving Spirit within you? That is a miracle! You have the light of the world inside your heart and mind and body, and through that Light, God can always see you. What joy that brings!

The Holy Spirit of grace desires to disturb your sleep. Blessed are you if you awaken. —Lars Linderot

Lord, thank you for blessing me with the miracle of your Holy Spirit…

Thankful for Hope

∞

You, who have shown me many troubles and calamities, / will revive me once more. / From the depths of the earth, / you will raise me up one more time.
—Psalm 71:20

What is hope about if it is not a hope that God will come to our aid when we're in trouble, that he will raise us up again when we are down? We have a benevolent Lord and Savior who offers us the hope of the cross and the hope of heaven. He looks at where we are and what we need and seeks to work toward our good. He always reminds us of our connection to him no matter where life takes us. We're redeemed with hope.

You are so precious to him that he delivers abundance packaged in grace and wrapped in love. He is the God of all things possible and through him and in him you are linked to the only real power in this universe. Bring all your cares and lay them at his feet and he will give you rest. Hope truly springs eternal!

If we were logical, the future would be bleak indeed. But we are more than logical. We are human beings, and we have faith, and we have hope. —Jacques Cousteau

Lord, my heart overflows with love and hope and gratitude …

WEEK 43/ DAY 2: 'Twas the Night Before Christmas

If we see what we hope for, that isn't hope. Who hopes for what they already see? But if we hope for what we don't see, we wait for it with patience. —Romans 8:24-25

Remember what it was like when you were a kid waiting for Santa on Christmas Eve? You had made a list or hinted strongly to your parents about the gifts you hoped would be under the tree on Christmas morning. That kind of child-like hope is something to hold on to as you wait patiently for the hope you have in your Lord.

Hope is itself a species of happiness, and perhaps the chief happiness which this world affords. —Samuel Johnson

Lord, thank you for the way that hope fills my heart…

WEEK 43/ DAY 3: Expect the Unexpected

Therefore, once you have your minds ready for action and you are thinking clearly, place your hope completely on the grace that will be brought to you when Jesus Christ is revealed. —1 Peter 1:13

What do you expect? Do you expect things to go well, to turn around if they aren't going so well just now, or to get better soon? God loves you so much that he waits for you to place all your concerns, all your hope, all your expectations squarely in his hand, and then he comes to help. Expect the unexpected goodness of God!

We love to expect, and when expectation is either disappointed or gratified, we want to be again expecting. —Samuel Johnson

Lord, thank you that I can expect good things from your loving hand…

WEEK 43/ DAY 4: *Faith, Hope, and Love*

May the God of hope fill you with all joy and peace in faith so that you overflow with hope by the power of the Holy Spirit.
—Romans 15:13

Are you overflowing with hope today? If not, maybe it's a simple matter of going back to the Source of your hope and letting him fill you with peace and joy, reminding you that he is with you all the way wherever you are and in whatever you hope to do. Praise the Lord!

The word "hope" I take for faith; and indeed hope is nothing else but the constancy of faith. —John Calvin

Lord, thank you for giving me the kind of hope that overflows...

WEEK 43/ DAY 5: *More Than a Little Hope*

Be happy in your hope, stand your ground when you're in trouble, and devote yourselves to prayer. —Romans 12:12

The thing about being hopeful, filling yourself up with hope and optimism, is that it tends to make you happy. It gives you every reason to keep going and believing and trusting that God is with you and is already working out the details of your concerns until you experience his good for you. Hope stands its ground with prayer and gratitude.

Optimism is the faith that leads to achievement. Nothing can be done without hope and confidence. —Helen Keller

Lord, thank you for helping me trust that I have every reason to be optimistic...

WEEK 43/ DAY 6: *Hope Dances with Courage*

We know that trouble produces endurance, endurance produces
character, and character produces hope. —Romans 5:3-4

Life is a dance and sometimes you're in the swing of it, gliding nicely across the floor, and sometimes you're at a stand-still waiting for the music to start again. The fact is that your partners for the dance, hope and courage, are always ready to help you move your feet once again.

He that lives in hope dances without the music. —George Herbert

Lord, thank you for keeping me in the dance of hope...

WEEK 43/ DAY 7: *Confident in Hope*

I pray that the eyes of your heart will have enough light to see
what is the hope of God's call, what is the richness of God's glori-
ous inheritance among believers. —Ephesians 1:18

When you have confidence in God's call on your life, knowing the full measure of all that you are in him, your hope becomes even more grounded. You know the truth and that truth truly sets you free. Your life then, abounds in hope. Thanks be to God!

The word which God has written on the brow of every person is hope.
—Victor Hugo

Lord, thank you that I have confidence in my hope in you...

Thankful for Adversity

Though the Lord gives you the bread of distress and the water of oppression, your teacher will no longer hide, but you will see your teacher. If you stray to the right or the left, you will hear a word that comes from behind you: "This is the way; walk in it."
—Isaiah 30:20-21

It's not really our nature to embrace adversity. If anything, we hope to get rid of it as soon as possible so we can smooth the waters and sail on without thinking or worry. Yet, it's the waves that bounce us around and cause us to come immediately into the present moment, that often have the most impact on helping us find real direction for our lives.

We may identify with Job when we're going through pain and misery. We may suffer the platitudes of friends who unwittingly assume we've done something to bring this sad situation on ourselves and that in some way we've merited it. Yet, we know that God sees us from a different perspective than our friends see us. He sees us differently than we see ourselves. He sees what we can become.

Sometimes, it's adversity that brings the best gift. It's the moment when things look the bleakest, when the storms are rising, that we truly discover our own strengths and the brightest light of possibility. We're in God's hands all the time, in peace and in adversity. Thank the Lord!

A smooth sea never made a skillful mariner, neither do uninterrupted prosperity and success qualify for usefulness and happiness. The storms of adversity, like those of the ocean, rouse the faculties, and excite the invention, prudence, skill and fortitude of the voyager. —Author unknown

Lord, thank you for being with me even in rough waters...

WEEK 44/ DAY 2: *Getting in the Game*

*Whoever isn't with me is against me, and whoever doesn't gather
with me scatters.* —Matthew 12:30

It may seem more comfortable to merely sit on the sidelines of life and not take any risks. After all, playing it safe might mean that you can keep control of things. The fact is, though, that God wants you to get in the game because that's where you can learn to be extraordinary. Nothing is more deadening to your soul then to be suited up and simply sit out the whole game.

All the blessings we enjoy are Divine deposits, committed to our trust on this condition, that they should be dispensed for the benefit of our neighbors. —John Calvin

Lord, thank you for getting me into the game of life, even when there are obstacles…

WEEK 44/ DAY 3: *Obstacle Courses*

*When you cry out, / let those things you've gathered save you! /
The wind will lift them all;/ one breath will take them away.*
—Isaiah 57:13

You may feel like your life is one long obstacle course. Everywhere you turn, there is one more hurdle to be jumped over, one more road block to be torn down. Yet, the fact is that God has prepared you more than you know to meet those obstacles. Beyond that, he is with you to help you overcome them.

Most of our obstacles would melt away if, instead of cowering before them, we should make up our minds to walk boldly through them. —Orison Swett Marden

Lord, thank you for being with me when I meet obstacles…

WEEK 44/ DAY 4: *Put Down the Load*

Come to me, all you who are struggling hard and carrying heavy loads, and I will give you rest. —Matthew 11:28

Sometimes we create our own adverse situations simply because we try too hard to carry the weight of our troubles all by ourselves. We forget that we aren't alone in our circumstances, but that God is truly in control. When adversity strikes you right in the heart, then turn your heart to your Savior.

It's not the load that breaks you down, it's the way you carry it.
—Author unknown

Lord, thank you for always being willing to carry my burdens...

WEEK 44/ DAY 5: *Anxiety Meditation*

Throw all your anxiety onto him, because he cares about you.
—1 Peter 5:7

It's common these days for people to take anxiety medication. We're so bombarded by life that we can't always bear it on our own strength. Perhaps the answer though is not to be medicated, but to be meditative and lean more heavily on the One who can make a real difference. We know that his power becomes even greater in our weakness.

Anxiety is the rust of life, destroying its brightness and weakening its power. A childlike and abiding trust in Providence is its best preventive and remedy.
—Author unknown

Lord, thank you for staying close to me at all times...

WEEK 44/ DAY 6: *Keep Your Eyes on the Prize*

So then let's also run the race that is laid out in front of us, since we have such a great cloud of witnesses surrounding us. Let's throw off any extra baggage, get rid of the sin that trips us up, and fix our eyes on Jesus, faith's pioneer and perfecter.
—Hebrews 12:1

The airlines aren't the only ones that cause you to pay for baggage these days. You pay for all the baggage, the weight of the world that you haul around from one place to the next. Don't make it harder to reach your own goals than you have to. Call out to Jesus and thank him for running the race with you.

To see God is the promised goal of all our actions and the promised height of all our joys. —Augustine of Hippo

Lord, thank you for lightening my load…

WEEK 44/ DAY 7: *Healing Broken Hearts*

The LORD is close to the brokenhearted; / he saves those whose spirits are crushed. / The righteous have many problems, / but the LORD delivers them from every one. —Psalm 34:18-19

Adversity may ultimately strengthen us, but it still doesn't feel good. In the midst of it, our hearts can be broken and our trials almost unbearable. The good news, though, is that God sees us even then, he sees us and seeks to deliver us from the things that would crush our spirits. Thanks be to God!

The saint never knows the joy of the Lord in spite of tribulation, but because of it.
—Oswald Chambers

Lord, thank you for delivering me from trials…

Thankful for Angels

Keep loving each other like family. Don't neglect to open up your homes to guests, because by doing this some have been hosts to angels without knowing it.
—Hebrews 13:1-2

It's probably safe to say that we don't truly understand the work of angels. We know that some of them are messengers who have appeared at divine moments in history to guide the way of our biblical ancestors. We know that an angel spent time with Mary as he shared the story of God's Son and how he would come to earth through her. We know shepherds and wise men were guided by them.

Yet, stories abound even in our current cultures that indicate angels are still with us. Most of us probably hope we have an angel guardian, some presence we become aware of from time to time, who watches over our daily lives and nudges us at moments we need extra help. Angels are beings created by God to serve him and to serve humankind. In that regard, then, it is only right that we offer thanks to our angels for being there even when we don't realize it, and for lifting us up according to God's command.

If you really think about it, you'll probably be able to recall a time or two when you would swear an angel was present in your life. You may have even entertained an angel in your home without knowing it. Thank your angels with great joy.

Beside each believer stands an angel as protector and shepherd leading him to life.
—Basil the Great

Lord, with a humble heart, I thank you for angels…

WEEK 45/ DAY 2: *GPS—God's Personal Servants*

*In the same way, I tell you, joy breaks out in the presence of God's
angels over one sinner who changes both heart and life.*
—Luke 15:10

Your guidance system on your car may well get you from one place to the
next, but the fact remains it will never be able to get you from earth to heaven;
only God can do that. Thanks to him, he's provided you with a lot of helpers,
sometimes through his Holy Spirit, sometimes through angels—anything he
can do to keep you safely on the journey.

*An angel can illumine the thought and mind of man by strengthening the power of
vision, and by bringing within his reach some truth which the angel himself contem-
plates.* —Thomas Aquinas

Lord, I am truly grateful for the guidance of angels…

WEEK 45/ DAY 3: *911 Angels*

My God sent his messenger, who shut the lions' mouths.
—Daniel 6:22

When Daniel was in trouble, he sent out an SOS, called 911, and tried to get
help however he could. He knew that he couldn't escape the lions' den without
some supernatural help. It didn't take long for God to dispatch a messenger or
two to come to his aid. He does the same thing for you. Call on him anytime
and he'll see that help comes quickly.

*The word "Angel" simply means "messenger." If angels are messengers, then some-
one, somewhere must be sending a message.* —Dan Schaeffer

Lord, thank you for your divine messengers…

WEEK 45/ DAY 4: *The Voice of an Angel*

I'm about to send a messenger in front of you to guard you on your way and to bring you to the place that I've made ready. Pay attention to him and do as he says. —Exodus 23:20-21

We have a tendency to romanticize angels, turning their work into that of cherubs and themes for beautiful artwork. The fact is that angels are powerful messengers of God and when they speak, it is God's intention for us to listen and to heed their voices. When the work is important, God sees to it that you have all you need to fulfill it, even through angel voices.

I heard a soft melodious voice, more pure and harmonious than any I had heard with my ears before; I believed it was the voice of an angel who spoke to the other angels. —John Woolman

Lord, thank you for angels who strive to make me hear…

WEEK 45/ DAY 5: *Dream Angels*

As he was thinking about this, an angel from the Lord appeared to him in a dream… —Matthew 1:20

God uses all our senses to reach us. If need be, he'll even give us insights in the middle of our dreams, sending angels to teach us or show us the way. Trust your dreams, for God can best guide you when your mind is fully at rest.

Millions of spiritual creatures walk the earth unseen, both when we wake and when we sleep. —John Milton

Lord, thank you for guiding me even as I sleep…

WEEK 45/ DAY 6: *Fear Not!*

The Lord's angel stood before them, the Lord's glory shone around them, and they were terrified. The angel said, "Don't be afraid!" —Luke 2:9-10

The appearance of an angel must be intimidating indeed, for nearly every biblical encounter begins with some form of the phrase "Fear not!" These beings who are so close to God's throne and his glory, hold his light and power in ways that humans cannot fully comprehend, and yet, they come to offer strength and love to God's precious children. What joy that brings!

In Scripture the visitation of an angel is always alarming; it has to begin by saying, "Fear not." The Victorian angel looks as if it were going to say, "There, there." —C. S. Lewis

Lord, thank you that you always know how to approach us…

WEEK 45/ DAY 7: *Ministering Spirits*

He said, "Father, if it's your will, take this cup of suffering away from me. However, not my will but your will must be done." Then a heavenly angel appeared to him and strengthened him. —Luke 22:42-43

Jesus was spent. He had given every ounce of strength to serve God. He had done all he could and went off to pray and rest in his Father's arms. Seeing his anguish, God sent an angel to strengthen him. When you are spent, know that if you need an angel, God will send one your way as well. He knows what you need even before you ask.

An angel is a spiritual creature created by God without a body for the service of Christendom and the church. —Martin Luther

Thank you, Lord, for angels who come to our aid when we are weary…

Thankful for Infinite Blessings

The earth has yielded its harvest. / God blesses us—our God blesses us! / Let God continue to bless us; / let the far ends of the earth honor him.
—*Psalm 67:6-7*

Sometimes we become a bit glib about the notion of counting our blessings. We might even come to expect that some things are not necessarily blessings as much as they are the result of our own hard work or the natural order of things. If we do get to a place where we actually discount those good things that happen to us, not qualifying them as blessings, we might want to think again.

God, the Creator, is the only One in charge, the only dispenser of real blessings. He's the one who knows you more than anyone else and embraces you in ways that help you make sense of life. He dispenses gifts of joy and blessing everywhere he chooses, but you are the only one who can acknowledge him for those gifts and honor him for his generosity and love. Yes, blessings should be counted, if indeed counting is truly possible, since it may well be an infinite thing. God showers you with his goodness, and when you offer him a yielded and grateful heart, he searches for even more ways to bring you joy. He wants you to enjoy the harvest of his goodness.

God is more anxious to bestow his blessings on us than we are to receive them.
—Augustine of Hippo

Lord, what joy it brings my heart to know of your great blessings…

WEEK 46/ DAY 2: *The Blessing of Ambition*

*Instead, desire first and foremost God's kingdom and God's right-
eousness, and all these things will be given to you as well.*
—Matthew 6:33

If you attempt to do things that are so big they scare you, you have an understanding of what it means to be blessed by ambition. It's the desire for a better
world and a better life and to really accomplish great deeds that drives people
with ambition. God blesses all your efforts anytime you start with him before
you start to hit the target of your goals.

Attempt great things for God, expect great things from God. —William Carey

Lord, thank you for blessing me with a certain ambition…

WEEK 46/ DAY 3: *The Art of Blessing*

*The Lord's blessing makes a person rich, and no trouble is added
to it.* —Proverbs 10:22

You know those times in your life when everything is coming up roses. You
almost are afraid to enjoy it because you don't want to do anything that will
bring trouble to your current circumstances. In order to raise the joy of blessings to an art form, though, you must acknowledge your joy and share your
humble gratitude.

*Art is a collaboration between God and the artist, and the less the artist does the bet-
ter.* —André Gide

Lord, your blessings are indeed a work of art…

WEEK 46/ DAY 4: *In Praise of Comfort*

When my anxieties multiply, your comforting calms me down.
—Psalm 94:19

We love being comfortable. We are grateful when we are in the comfortable spaces of our own homes, or the warm embraces of our friends, or when we're receiving strength and comfort from our beloved Father in Heaven. The closer we draw to God, the more comfort he can offer us.

When spiritual comfort is sent to you by God, take it humbly and give thanks meekly for it. But know for certain that it is the great goodness of God that sends it to you, and not because you deserve it. —Thomas à Kempis

Lord, what a blessing it is to receive your comfort...

WEEK 46/ DAY 5: *The Friendship Blessing*

And Jonathan and David made a covenant together because Jonathan cared about David as much as he cared about himself.
—1 Samuel 18:3

What more can we ask of friendship than that it be about mutual caring and trust? The blessing of that kind of friendship is beyond measure, for it comes without individual agendas; it is a love like no others. May you always give thanks to God for the real friends who come your way.

Do not keep the alabaster boxes of your love and tenderness sealed up until your friends are dead. Fill their lives with sweetness. Speak approving cheering words while their ears can hear them and while their hearts can be thrilled by them.
—Henry Ward Beecher

Lord, thank you for the friends who make such a difference in my life...

WEEK 46/ DAY 6: *God's Goodness*

Praise the LORD! / Give thanks to the LORD because he is good, / because his faithful love endures forever. / Who could possibly repeat all of the LORD's mighty acts / or publicly recount all his praise? —Psalm 106:1-2

It's because God cannot be anything but good that you are the recipient of so many blessings. He seeks always for you to know that he works all things together simply to give you the best possible outcome. He blesses your life moment by moment. Praise him for his good and Holy Spirit.

God often takes a course for accomplishing His purposes directly contrary to what our narrow views would prescribe. He brings a death upon our feelings, wishes, and prospects when He is about to give us the desire of our hearts. —John Newton

Lord, my heart is humbled by your unending goodness to me…

WEEK 46/ DAY 7: *The Blessing of Knowing God*

The people who know the celebratory shout are truly happy! / They walk in the light of your presence, LORD! / They rejoice in your name all day long / and are uplifted by your righteousness / because you are the splendor of their strength. —Psalm 89:15-17

God knows you, and when you commit to him and come to know him, he walks with you and blesses your life. He gives you strength and renews your spirit whenever you choose to draw near. Praise his name!

Once you become aware that the main business that you are here for is to know God, most of life's problems fall into place of their own accord. —J. I. Packe

Lord, what a blessing it is to strive to know more of you…

Thankful for Courage

❧

All you who wait for the LORD, be strong and let your heart take courage.
—Psalm 31:24

"Have courage," we're told by friends and family, bible authors, and people we work with. Perhaps, then, it helps to have a picture of courage. Are you courageous like a superhero, ready to don your cape and head into the thick of battle, getting rid of the enemies? Are you like the cowardly lion in *The Wizard of Oz* feeling more like you need to have someone else give you a badge of courage?

Certainly, you haven't lived this long without recognizing that life is full of opportunities that require you to show up with a great amount of courage. You may be newly divorced or widowed and forced back into the search for a new partner. That takes courage! You may be looking for a new job and have to move to a new city, start life over, make new friends, find a new church—that takes courage! Perhaps you're battling a chronic illness or depression—courage, courage, courage!

The truth is your faith in God is built on your willingness to let go of fear and embrace courage. Most of life seems geared toward seeing how we do with that particular message. Let go of fear; trust God! Those words are simple, but they are packed with power and only you and God can embrace them in a way that makes all things possible. Fear not! Trust! Take heart, the Lord is with you!

Courage is the best gift of all; courage stands before everything. It is what preserves our liberty, safety, life, and our homes and parents, our country and our children. Courage comprises all things: a person with courage has every blessing. —Plautus

Lord, thank you for leading me toward greater courage…

WEEK 47/ DAY 2: *The Trust Walk*

The LORD is my solid rock, my fortress, my rescuer. / My God is my rock— / I take refuge in him!—he's my shield, my salvation's strength, my place of safety. —Psalm 18:2

You awaken each day and go on a trust walk. You may not identify it as such, but everything you do requires you to anchor yourself to the one true power of the universe, the God who made you and desires only your good. Thank him each day that you can trust him completely with your life.

In God alone there is faithfulness and faith in the trust that we may hold to him, on his promise and to his guidance. To hold to God is to rely on the fact that God is there for me, and to live in this certainty. —Karl Barth

Lord, thank you for being there for me each day…

WEEK 47/ DAY 3: *Courage and Faith*

Jesus said to him, " 'If you can do anything'? All things are possible for the one who has faith." At that the boy's father cried out, "I have faith; help my lack of faith!" —Mark 9:23-24

Imagine what it would be like to actually have the courage of your faith, to believe and trust so much that you could gather up your five smooth stones to slay a giant bully or wrestle with an angel. Thank God that he works with you right where you are to give you opportunities to grow in faith and courage.

Belief consists in accepting the affirmations of the soul; unbelief, in denying them. —Ralph Waldo Emerson

Lord, thank you that I'm learning to be more courageous in my faith…

WEEK 47/ DAY 4: *Do It Anyway!*

*There is no fear in love, but perfect love drives out fear, because
fear expects punishment. The person who is afraid has not been
made perfect in love.* —1 John 4:18

Remember the first time you struggled with fear? You were trying to take
your first step, or you went to kindergarten, or you tried out for a team, or had
some goal you were slightly afraid to go after. The blessing came when you did
it anyway, in spite of the fear, and learned you could. Thank God each time he
helps you overcome a fear and do what you aim to do.

*We gain strength, and courage, and confidence by each experience in which we really
stop to look fear in the face.… We must do that which we think we cannot.*
—Eleanor Roosevelt

Lord, thank you for giving me the courage to go after the goals I've set…

WEEK 47/ DAY 5: *Facing the Truth*

When the Spirit of Truth comes, he will guide you in all truth.
—John 16:13

Most of us live a sort of "Truth or Consequences" kind of life. We strive to
tell the truth, but are often comfortable with our own variations on the theme.
It seems that our truth is more important than someone else's truth. The fact
remains that the Spirit of Truth is the only direct and accurate source we have
for engaging in real truth-telling. We have so much to learn.

*If you don't learn and know your truths, you cannot speak them. If you don't speak
them, you will know a prison within. Tell your truths to yourself, and then to the others.
The truth really will set you free!* —Author unknown

Lord, thank you for being all truth and helping me to face the truth with
courage…

WEEK 47 / DAY 6: *I'm on a Mission!*

Then I heard the Lord's voice saying, "Whom should I send, and who will go for us?" I said, "I'm here; send me." —Isaiah 6:8

It takes courage to answer God's call on your life. It takes almost supernatural strength to say those words, "Send me, send me!" Yet, God has called and each day we choose to answer or not. Each day the mission is set and the work remains to be done. Thank God he has a mission for you.

I will go down, if you will hold the ropes. —William Carey

Lord, help me have the courage to carry out my mission for you…

WEEK 47 / DAY 7: *The Courage to Love Again and Again*

May the Lord cause you to increase and enrich your love for each other and for everyone in the same way as we also love you. May the love cause your hearts to be strengthened, to be blameless in holiness. —1 Thessalonians 3:12-13

Though love seems like it should be easy, it's actually hard work requiring more of you at times than you even wanted to give. If you equate the work of love to God's love for humankind, loving us in spite of us, then it's easier to understand the courage it takes to attract and sustain love again and again. Thank God for his great love lessons.

May God give you the courage to love others as he loves you—unconditionally! —Karen Moore

Lord, thank you for giving me the courage to keep loving others…

Thankful for Faith

Faith is the reality of what we hope for, the proof of what we don't see. The elders in the past were approved because they showed faith.
—Hebrews 11:1-2

A s you read through the stories of those hand-picked patriarchs and every-day people of biblical times, you might feel impressed with the way humans have been striving to get it right with God. The people mentioned in Hebrews are examples of what God can do in the life of a person who is faithful to his calling. Perhaps when you finish the reading, you wonder if your name will one day be added to the list, if somehow you might be an example for generations to come.

Be thankful for the faith you already have. God is working things out with you and every time you're willing to accept more of him, he'll be there. This is your time to shine, your time to reflect his Spirit to others who still seek to know him like you do.

Your faith helps God to see you and count all your efforts to righteousness. Hallelujah! God is good!

God does not keep an extra supply of goodness that is higher than faith, and there is no help at all in anything that is below it. Within faith is where the Lord wants us to stay. —Julian of Norwich

Lord, thank you for keeping me grounded in my faith…

WEEK 48/ DAY 2: *A Little Mustard-Seed Faith*

I assure you that if you have faith the size of a mustard seed, you could say to this mountain, "Go from here to there," and it will go. There will be nothing that you can't do. —Matthew 17:20

Imagine, a tiny speck of faith and you could move mountains! The fact that we don't often see the mountains getting up and moving around might make us believe that Jesus didn't mean that literally, and yet, how would we know? You can move mountains in your own life or community or job, all for the good of others anytime you choose to apply some mustard seed faith.

I seek not for a faith that will move a mountain, but for faith that will somehow move me. —Author unknown

Lord, thank you for all the ways you seek to move me to greater faith…

❧

WEEK 48/ DAY 3: *Faith and Worry*

Who among you by worrying can add a single moment to your life? —Matthew 6:27

If you can catch yourself in a worry, you might be able to stop it right on the spot by holding up your banner of faith. Sometimes you don't realize you're giving worry so much time, until it robs you of your peace and joy. Faith holds up the light, striving to show you the way through any darkness that worry may bring.

Tomorrow has two handles: the handle of fear and the handle of faith. You can take hold of it by either handle. —Author unknown

Lord, thank you for the faith that helps me cast worry aside…

WEEK 48/ DAY 4: *Faith in Baby Steps*

When I was a child, I used to speak like a child, reason like a child, think like a child. But now that I have become a man, I've put an end to childish things. —1 Corinthians 13:11

Thank God for every step of your path to grow in faith. He began his work in you from the moment you were born and he knows when you're ready to take yet another step closer to all he has for you. His faith in you abounds. Thank him for what he's given you so far.

Let us step into the darkness and reach out for the hand of God. The path of faith and darkness is so much safer than the one we would choose by sight.
—George MacDonald

Lord, thank you for being with me every step of the way…

WEEK 48/ DAY 5: *Faith Forward*

Therefore, let's draw near with a genuine heart with the certainty that our faith gives us, since our hearts are sprinkled clean from an evil conscience and our bodies are washed with pure water.
—Hebrews 10: 22

You may wonder at times if you have everything you need to make it through another day, to go forward with life. You may wonder at the abundance of God's provision. The fact is that faith is a matter of being in awe and wonder toward the One who draws you near, desiring for you to grow and move forward with him.

Faith is a foretaste of the knowledge that will make us blessed in this life to come.
—Thomas Aquinas

Lord, let me gratefully go forward in faith…

WEEK 48/ DAY 6: *Acting in Faith*

Someone might claim, "You have faith and I have action." But how can I see your faith apart from your actions? Instead, I'll show you my faith by putting it into practice in faithful action.
—James 2:18

It's gratifying to be around people who put their faith into action, who practice what they preach. The opportunity for such things is not available everywhere in the world without serious consequences. How blessed you are to be able to freely practice your faith.

If faith produces no works, I see / That faith is not a living tree. / Thus faith and works together grow / For a separate life, they cannot know.
—Hannah More (adapted)

Lord, thank you that I'm free to practice my faith every day…

WEEK 48/ DAY 7: *With a Little Faith and Love*

Faith working through love does matter. —Galatians 5:6

It's worth noting that faith and love are not things you can purchase in a store, save up in a bank, or take pride in. They are both matters of the heart and how you express these gifts makes a difference to everyone you know. God bless you as you grow in faith and love.

God shows himself not to reason, but to faith and love. Faith is an organ of knowledge, and love is an organ of experience. To know God is not through reason, nor is it through emotions, but by faith and love. —A. W. Tozer

Lord, thank you for a faith in my heart that can express itself through love…

Thankful for Birthdays

❧

*A person's steps are made secure by the LORD / when they delight
in his way. / Though they trip up, they won't be thrown down, /
because the LORD holds their hand. / I was young and now I'm
old, but I have never seen the righteous left all alone.*
—Psalm 37:23-25

R emember when you were excited that your birthday was coming? You
told everyone that you were turning five or that you were finally sixteen
and could drive a car. You were thrilled to be twenty-one and then slowly, the
birthday fun seemed to ebb a little as you reached thirty and then forty and
finally what probably didn't feel like fabulous fifty.

Turn your thoughts around and celebrate each birthday as the privilege it
really is, as the opportunity to keep growing and loving and digging into life.
Birthdays are God's way of suggesting you're not quite ready to come back to
base camp, you still have work to do for him. Count the blessings you hold dear
and stand up with joy to announce your excitement at your next birthday. Give
thanks to God that you mean so much to him that he counts all your days as
opportunities to get to know you better.

Your heart is ageless and your spirit is eternal. Praise the Lord!

*It would be a good thing if young people were wise and old people were strong, but
God has arranged things better.* —Martin Luther

Lord, I am truly grateful for every day and every year you give me…

WEEK 49/ DAY 2: *In Praise of Childhood*

No doubt about it: / children are a gift from the LORD; / the fruit of the womb is a divine reward. / The children born when one is young / are like arrows in the hand of a warrior. —Psalm 127:3-4

You were born for a purpose, and as a child you were a great gift to your family. You may not have known that at the time, you may not have realized what you meant to everyone around you, but God did. He wanted you to be loved and nourished and so he provided you with a family.

I love little children, and it is not a slight thing when they who are fresh from God, love us. —Charles Dickens

Lord, thank you for my childhood...

WEEK 49/ DAY 3: *Twixt Twelve and Twenty*

Rejoice, young person, while you are young! Your heart should make you happy in your prime. —Ecclesiastes 11:9

Ah, remember those birthday milestones, the ones that turned you into a teenager, made you feel indestructible and strong, part adult and part child? Those were exploring years, growing and becoming, forming the building blocks of your future. Thank God he watched over you so well during those years.

When I was a boy of 14, my father was so ignorant I could hardly stand to have the old man around. But when I got to be 21, I was astonished at how much the old man had learned in seven years. —Mark Twain

Lord, thank you for guarding and guiding my teenage years...

WEEK 49/ DAY 4: *Thirty-Something*

Remember your creator in your prime, / before the days of trouble arrive, /and those years, about which you'll say, "I take no pleasure in these." —Ecclesiastes 12:1

The light of your birthday candles is growing a bit bolder, reminding you of time and its stubborn persistent passage. You've been too busy with life to really notice because you're still becoming, still moving up God's ladder of success. God is with you and what joy that brings!

If you are pleased with what you are, you have stopped already. If you say, "It is enough," you are lost. Keep on walking, moving forward, trying for the goal. —Augustine of Hippo

Lord, I thank you for your hand in all that I am...

WEEK 49/ DAY 5: *Forty? Seriously?*

Teach us to number our days so we can have a wise heart. —Psalm 90:12

Forty candles, and with them comes the dawn, the dawning revelation that life moves quickly and change continues. This is the year of God's opportunity to allow you to reimagine yourself, reinvent your life, and revisit your spirit. It's time to welcome greater shades of wisdom.

Dost thou love life? Then do not squander time, for that is the stuff life is made of. —Benjamin Franklin

Lord, I am so thankful for the time you have given me...

WEEK 49/ DAY 6: *Birthdays in the Middle*

*In your perspective a thousand years / are like yesterday past, like
a short period during the night watch. / You sweep humans away
like a dream, / like grass that is renewed in the morning.*
—Psalm 90:4-5

Experience has blessed you with insight and the truth that life does not go
on forever, that celebrating another birthday truly is a gift from God. You know
more than anything that now is the time to make life count, to follow your
dreams and fulfill your purpose. Sing God's praise!

At fifty, everyone has the face he deserves. —George Orwell

Lord, thank you for lighting the way to each new day...

WEEK 49/ DAY 7: *Thank God for Another Birthday!*

*I came so that they could have life—indeed, so that they could
live life to the fullest.* —John 10:10

As you turn out the lights to appreciate the glow of another birthday celebration, you are touched by the bright smiles and love on the faces of those who
celebrate with you. You are awed to be here, still growing and becoming.
Thank God for his incredible love and investment into your life today.

*The one who is happiest, lives from day to day and asks no more, garnering the sim-
ple goodness of life.* —Euripides (adapted)

Lord, thank you for my many birthdays, what a gift they are...

Thankful for Salvation

You are saved by God's grace because of your faith. This salvation is God's gift. It's not something you possessed. It's not something you did that you can be proud of. Instead, we are God's accomplishment, created in Christ Jesus to do good things. God planned for these good things to be the way that we live our lives.
—Ephesians 2:8-10

A re you awed to think of yourself as God's accomplishment? You are his workmanship, his idea and design. He knew you before you were in your mother's womb and he has an incredible plan for your life. He sees you and knows you. You're always on a first-name basis with him. Along with your life, your mini-visit to earth, God planned your return to him, the way to come back to your heavenly home when your visit is over. He wants you to be able to take the lessons you learned on earth and share them with him in great joy for all eternity.

God plans only and always for your good. He loves to see you thrive, to see you grow and change. He loves to see your heart soften toward him and toward those around you. Your salvation is a portion of your life; and through his grace, your name is in the guestbook, your reservation was made ahead of time. Thank the Lord!

God just doesn't throw a life preserver to a drowning person. He goes to the bottom of the sea, and pulls a corpse from the bottom of the sea, takes him up on the bank, breathes into him the breath of life and makes him alive. That's what the Bible says happens in your salvation. —R. C. Sproul

Lord, I am humbled by the gift of your saving grace…

WEEK 50/ DAY 2: *Saints and Sinners*

*This saying is reliable and deserves full acceptance: "Christ Jesus came into the world to save sinners" —and I'm the biggest sinner of all. —*1 Timothy 1:15

Perhaps you can relate to Paul's sense that he might be the biggest sinner of all. After all, you realize that you are far from sainthood. The beauty of God's grace and mercy, though, is that sin is sin; big or small, horrible or foolish, it's all the same and it all requires the same action, faith in Jesus. Thank God he sets you free.

The best and brightest of God's saints is but a poor mixed being. —J. C. Ryle

Lord, my heart is humbled by your willingness to save me…

WEEK 50/ DAY 3: *Save Me, Save Me!*

Like sheep we had all wandered away, / each going its own way, / but the LORD let fall on him all our crimes. —Isaiah 53:6

There's nothing quite as sobering as the realization that God saved us even before we knew we needed to be saved. Even though we strayed, kept walking away, doing our own thing, he reached out and rescued us. Glory be to God!

Salvation is so simple we can overlook it, so profound we can never comprehend it. —Author unknown

Lord, thank you for saving me even when I walked away…

WEEK 50/ DAY 4: *Salvation for the Struggling*

We know that the Law is spiritual, but I'm made of flesh and blood, and I'm sold as a slave to sin. I don't know what I'm doing, because I don't do what I want to do. Instead, I do the thing that I hate. —Romans 7:14-15

God knows you need his help, not only to work out salvation, but to live fully in his grace and mercy. Your humanness gets in the way of what you hope to be, what you desire. God chose you to be faithful and to believe that he is with you in every struggle. His love saves you every time!

God is none other than the Savior of our wretchedness. So we can only know God well by knowing our iniquities.... Those who have known God without knowing their wretchedness have not glorified him, but have glorified themselves. —Blaise Pascal

Lord, I can't thank you enough for saving me from my unworthy self…

WEEK 50/ DAY 5: *The Name of Salvation*

Salvation can be found in no one else. Throughout the whole world, no other name has been given among humans through which we must be saved. —Acts 4:12

The religions of the world all have leaders who sought to know God. Some of them turned themselves into gods, some stumbled upon the true God of the universe by another path, and some still seek him. For Christians, the fact remains that Jesus is indeed the only name we've been given that offers us a bridge from here to eternity. Thank God for his Son!

Jesus was God spelling himself out in language humanity could understand. —S. D. Gordon

Lord, thank you for spelling your name so my heart could understand…

WEEK 50/ DAY 6: *Salvation Power*

I'm not ashamed of the gospel: it is God's own power for salvation to all who have faith in God. —Romans 1:16

Power and weakness walk hand in hand. Both are yours through your faith in God. His power through you is made stronger when you are willing to yield your heart, rest at his feet, and give him the opportunity to know you. Because of him, you are more powerful than you know—always.

All the resources of the Godhead are at our disposal. —Jonathan Goforth

Lord, I don't always understand the power of salvation, but I'm humbled and grateful...

WEEK 50/ DAY 7: *God So Loved!*

God so loved the world that he gave his only Son, so that everyone who believes in him won't perish but will have eternal life.
—John 3:16

God did it out of love! He saw you and wanted you to be able to return safely home. He wanted you to have a life that was full and blessed. God's Son is your light, your salvation, your perfect path to peace. Hallelujah!

Everything comes from love, all is ordained for the salvation of man. God does nothing without this goal in mind. —Catherine of Siena

Lord, your love is my refuge and joy...

Thankful for Temptation

No temptation has seized you that isn't common for people. But God is faithful. He won't allow you to be tempted beyond your abilities. Instead, with the temptation, God will also supply a way out so that you will be able to endure it.
—1 Corinthians 10:13

*H*old on, you're probably thinking. *Are you serious that I should be grateful for those things that tempt me and often cause me to fail?* Consider some of the greatest lessons of your life, the ones that caused you to seek after God more fervently, that caused you to quake at your very core because you're so ashamed of what you discovered about yourself. Those lessons came because you were tempted by something, tempted to walk past your own boundaries, close your eyes momentarily to consequences, and move mindlessly forward. Temptations are often the best teachers you will have and the ones that can most quickly bring you to your knees. They play on your pride and your ego, they confuse your spirit and your mind, and they entice you into an unfavorable path.

Gratitude comes not so much from succumbing to those temptations, but from the realization of your own need for Jesus.

Whatever good is to be attained, struggle is necessary. So do not fear temptations, but rejoice in them, for they lead to achievement. God helps and protects you.
—St. Barsanuphius

Lord, thank you that I've discovered more of you and more about myself through temptations...

WEEK 51 / DAY 2: *Caving in to Temptation*

Wisdom begins with the fear of the LORD, / but fools despise wisdom and instruction. —Proverbs 1:7

You know what's right. You learned right from wrong a long time ago. Your heart beats louder trying to remind you of the truth, trying to keep you from falling. Nevertheless, even with a cacophony of trumpet blasts, you fall down. Thank God he knows right where to pick you up.

We usually know what we can do, but temptation shows us who we are. —Thomas à Kempis

Lord, thank you for loving me through my worst failures…

WEEK 51 / DAY 3: *Lead Us Not into Temptation*

No one who is tested should say, "God is tempting me!" This is because God is not tempted by any form of evil, nor does he tempt anyone. —James 1:13

The supermarket to temptation never seems to close. You can drive by it at 2 AM and find opportunities there. You can pretend it doesn't exist and it will nag at you until you walk back through its doors. God doesn't tempt you to do wrong. He asks you to come to him when temptation beckons.

The voice of Christ: Write My words in your heart and meditate on them earnestly, for in time of temptation they will be very necessary. —Thomas à Kempis

Lord, thank you for being with me any time I feel temptation looming…

WEEK 51/ DAY 4: *Finding the Escape Hatch*

The Lord knows how to rescue the godly from their trials, and how to keep the unrighteous for punishment on the Judgment Day. —2 Peter 2:9

It can feel like you're so driven by the thing that tempts you that you might as well be soaring through space in a small capsule, because any way you turn the temptation is there. It seems bigger than you are, pulling you like some gravitational force to cause you to sin. Thank God he has provided an escape hatch.

Unwillingness to accept God's "way of escape" from temptation frightens me—what a rebel yet resides within. —Jim Elliot

Lord, thank you for providing a way out when I feel tempted …

WEEK 51/ DAY 5: *Save Me from Myself*

Everyone is tempted by their own cravings; they are lured away and enticed by them. Once those cravings conceive, they give birth to sin. —James 1:14-15

The more you understand about yourself and the closer you draw near to God, the more you can resist those crazy times when temptations can lure you. When you're depressed by life's circumstances, deprived of love or self-worth, you're vulnerable. Thank God, he strengthens you with every effort you make to be near him.

The best way to drive out the devil, if he will not yield to texts of scripture, is to jeer and flout him, for he cannot stand scorn. —Martin Luther

Lord, thank you for staying close to me even when I feel tempted…

WEEK 51/ DAY 6: *Please Close the Door!*

And don't lead us into temptation, but rescue us from the evil one.
—Matthew 6:13

If you could get God to simply close the door on temptation, that might seem like a good way out. After all, if you're simply not tempted, then you won't run the risk of getting into any difficulty. The fact is that God loves you so much, he gives you choices all the time. Thankfully, he stays with you no matter what you choose.

Temptation usually comes in through a door that has deliberately been left open.
—Author unknown

Lord, thank you for knowing me so well and helping me…

WEEK 51/ DAY 7: *Tempting Morsels*

Go in through the narrow gate. The gate that leads to destruction is broad and the road wide, so many people enter through it.
—Matthew 7:13

You may wonder who left the gate open to every possible form of temptation. You can usually resist the big temptations. It's the little ones that will wear you down. TV commercials tempt you to believe that almost nothing about you is okay. They hope you'll bite on this idea and buy their products. God's hope is that you'll remember who you are in him.

Let us learn more about the power of temptation in order to avoid it.
—John Owen

Lord, thank you for giving me wisdom to help me overcome temptations…

WEEK 52/ DAY 1

Thankful for God

❦

God said to Moses, "I Am Who I Am. So say to the Israelites, 'I Am has sent me to you.'" God continued, "Say to the Israelites, 'The LORD, the God of your ancestors, Abraham's God, Isaac's God, and Jacob's God, has sent me to you.' This is my name forever; this is how all generations will remember me."
—*Exodus 3:14-15*

As we embark on this week, let us be very intentional about our thanks and praise for God—not *to* God, but *for* God. When God introduced himself to Moses and the children of Israel, he tried to help them understand that he would reign as God forever and ever. There were no other gods.

Our lives are built around the beliefs we hold about the God of the universe. We go to him when we're in trouble as he invited us to do. We go to him in prayer and praise and in gratitude for our lives. We go to him when we are angry or disappointed or simply confused by all that is. We go to him when we're afraid and we need to be consoled and we need to be connected to the true living source of all that is good. We are grateful to God for countless things, and that thanks starts by being grateful that God exists.

There is a God-shaped vacuum in the heart of every person which cannot be filled by any created thing, but only by God, the Creator, made known through Jesus.
—Blaise Pascal

God of the universe, though I do not truly comprehend you, I know you're there and I thank you...

WEEK 52/ DAY 2: *Creator God*

When God began to create the heavens and the earth—the earth was without shape or form, it was dark over the deep sea, and God's wind swept over the waters—God said, "Let there be light." And so light appeared. God saw how good the light was.
—Genesis 1:1-4

God didn't rise above the ranks of some unknown alien world to become the Creator of this earth and this universe. God existed before all time and thought. God is unexplainable from human timelines and standards, and yet every aspect of his work touches our lives.

The world forgets you, its creator, and falls in love with what you have created instead of with you. —Augustine of Hippo

God, thank you for knowing me long before I knew you...

WEEK 52/ DAY 3: *Because God Exists*

Ever since the creation of the world, God's invisible qualities— God's eternal power and divine nature—have been clearly seen, because they are understood through the things God has made. So humans are without excuse. —Romans 1:20

God has made it nearly impossible for us to miss the fact of his presence. He put himself into everything he made and knew that it was good. He knew that we could see him in the beauty of rich landscapes, rushing waterfalls, and grand mountaintops. He knew that if we looked anywhere, we could find him.

The conclusion we reach in our reflection on this question [of the existence of God] has the most momentous consequences in the orientation of our thinking and our daily living. —Edward Sillem

Lord God, thank you for being all that is...

WEEK 52/ DAY 4: *God's Radiance and Glory*

When Judas was gone, Jesus said, "Now the Human One has been glorified, and God has been glorified in him. If God has been glorified in him, God will also glorify the Human One in himself and will glorify him immediately." —John 13:31-32

We don't use a word like *glory* very often. We may understand it in a sense of winning a prize or receiving some special recognition, but when it comes to God, we don't know the half of it. Giving God the glory he deserves may not even be possible in our human condition, but praising him with humble hearts pleases him anyway.

For though we very truly hear that the kingdom of God will be filled with splendor, joy, happiness and glory, yet when these things are spoken of, they remain utterly remote from our perception, and as it were, wrapped in obscurities. —John Calvin

Lord, I thank you for any chance to bring you true worship and praise…

WEEK 52/ DAY 5: *God Is Holy*

Holy, holy, holy / is the LORD of heavenly forces! / All the earth / is filled with God's glory! —Isaiah 6:3

We strive to be more of the image of God in all that we do. We know that we cannot come close to him unless we, too, are holy. That holiness enters us via the Son and the Holy Spirit. God has found a way to help us be more like him, to be true heirs of holiness.

A holy life will produce the deepest impression. Lighthouses blow no horns; they only shine. —Dwight L. Moody

Lord, I thank you for guiding me into a life that is more holy…

WEEK 52/ DAY 6: *God's Mercy*

The LORD your God is merciful and compassionate. He won't
withdraw his presence from you if you return to him.
—2 Chronicles 30:9

Gratitude springs from the heart of anyone who seeks God's forgiveness, his mercy and compassion. When no one else can console you or give you peace, than God invites you to come to him. He will be with you any time you ask.

There's a wideness in God's mercy /like the wideness of the sea; / there's a kindness in God's justice, / which is more than liberty. —F. W. Faber

Lord, I am truly grateful for your mercy and kindness...

WEEK 52/ DAY 7: *What Is God?*

I am the alpha and the omega, the first and the last, the beginning
and the end. —Revelation 22:13

We try so hard to imagine God as a kindly grandfather that we seldom reflect on the fact that God is supernatural. He is not flesh and blood. He is not male or female. He is an entity, a being unlike any that our minds can understand. However, he is also the "person" of God who invites us to have a loving relationship with him.

God is incorporeal, immaterial, impalpable, beyond quantity and circumscription, beyond form and figure. —Cyril of Alexandria

God, though I may not recognize your outward appearance, my soul gratefully bears witness to your loving heart...